P9-EAY-060

Contents

Foreword   *vii*

Chapter I \ THE POWER OF THE FEDERAL GOVERNMENT   *3*

Chapter II \ THE INFLUENCE OF TEACHERS ORGANIZATIONS   25

Chapter III \ THE ROLE OF OTHER NATIONAL ORGANIZA- TIONS   *46*

Chapter IV \ STATE GOVERNMENT AND STATEWIDE GROUPS   79

Chapter V \ THE THEORY AND PRACTICE OF LOCAL CON- TROL   *118*

Chapter VI \ RESTORING A BALANCE OF POWERS IN EDUCA- TION   *155*

Appendix   *175*

Notes   *197*

Index   *203*

Who Controls American Education?

Who Controls American Education?

A GUIDE FOR LAYMEN

BY JAMES D. KOERNER

BEACON

PRESS

BOSTON

Foreword

"THE FIRST CONDITION of progress," as Albert Jay Nock once remarked, "is a lively and peremptory dissatisfaction." He had a good deal of such dissatisfaction himself, especially in regard to American education. Because many other people are similarly dissatisfied these days, it would seem to follow that progress is also being made. I don't know whether it is or not, but I think the time has come for laymen to concern themselves with more than particular deficiencies in the curriculum or the standards of their schools. They need to be concerned with the way in which education is governed in the United States.

If you ask an American the question, "Who controls American education?" you will probably get a vague and confused answer. Or none. Most people don't know who controls American education because little attention has been given the question by either educators or the public. Also because the question is not easily or neatly answered. Authority and influence are widely distributed in education and are exercised in ways that do not lend themselves to precise analysis. Yet the problem of how education is controlled is more important than most of the other educational problems that concern Americans.

People worry about whether Johnny can read or Susy can figure, or whether teachers are well trained and properly selected, or maybe whether discipline is good, or textbooks adequate. Few people carry their concern beyond the particular to the general question, much more important, of how decisions get made in education in the first place. If they think about it at all, they are apt to think of the local school board as the chief means of control—and they would be wrong. Who really decides how Johnny will be taught to read? Or the way in which teachers will be trained? Or what textbooks will be used? Or what the goals and priorities of the local schools should be?

The field of education, even though it consumes a giant's share of the nation's resources, has until recently received little political analysis. Now, however, the complicated process by which policy is made seems to have engaged the interest of a number of sociologists, political scientists, and professional educators. This new subject of study has come to be called "the politics of education" and is achieving such popularity that it may soon become another academic bandwagon of the sort that come and go with great frequency in our educational system.

The public itself has also shown some interest in our educational politics, largely because of weaknesses in the present system of control. People in and out of education are not at all happy with the traditional methods by which decisions get made. The old way, they feel, cannot cope with such urgent problems as racial segregation, ghetto education, the rapid urbanization or suburbanization of the country, highly unequal resources among the cities and states, the dehumanization of mass-produced higher education, and the interaction of economic, social, and judicial decisions of national scope.

Public interest in "the politics of education" has also grown out of the frustrations of people who want to see reforms made in education but who see them constantly blocked by the rigidities of a well entrenched bureaucracy. So they then turn their attention to the problem of how to gain political leverage in education and of how radical change can be made in schools. After a decade of work in educational reform, James Bryant Conant remarked in a 1967 interview:

If I were twenty years younger, and had the ideas I have now, I would go and sit in Albany as a lobbyist, and see to it that the bills to support public schools and reform teacher education got through the legislature. Political action is what's needed.[1]

Little has yet come of the formalized, "scientific" study of how education is controlled, perhaps because so few instruments exist with which to measure the exercise of power. I have reviewed most of the academic studies in the field and have found some of them helpful in supplying simple information; but none of them has been strong in analysis or conclusions. Even the information in these studies is frequently conflicting and based on simplistic questionnaires or dubious interviewing techniques.

The value of these formal studies is, alas, further diminished by their jawbreaking jargon. The habit of inventing a special vocabulary with which to give status to every subspecialty that comes along is bad enough in the academic departments of our colleges and universities; in professional education it is a compulsion. Hence these studies of educational politics are studded with impenetrable paragraphs and hideous coinages often invented at random by their authors and then picked up by other authors. "Key influentials" abound in these studies, never merely "important people." So do "power-wielders," "demand articulators," and "change agents." There is a lot of talk about things like "power structure research theories," "pluralistic participatory centers," "polylithic power constructs," and various kinds of "sociometry" ("mass," "elite," "decision," etc.). There are innumerable passages like "The long-awaited proponent victory must be viewed in the context of several inextricably interrelated factors."

An extended exposure to swamp gas of this kind is not merely a punishing experience that does nothing to strengthen one's faith in the academic study of how American education is controlled; even worse, one may become infected oneself through sheer exposure—in which case I can only crave my reader's pardon.

This book makes no pretense to being a scientific or even a systematic inquiry. I have sent no questionnaires, gathered no "raw data," erected no "construct theories," computed no co-efficients of correlation. Instead I have given careful consideration to what other people have done in the politics of education and have put it together with my own experience and, if you like, my prejudices. The result is a kind of extended essay addressed to the layman in which the essential elements of the government of education in America are discussed along with what I think is strong and weak, right and wrong, in the present system.

I am indebted to a number of friends and associates for reading the book in manuscript and giving me their uninhibited criticism: Mrs. Talcott Bates, a distinguished member of the State Board of Education in California from 1960 to 1968; Mrs. Barry Bingham, vice president of the Louisville *Courier-Journal* and president of the Council for Basic Education; Mortimer Smith, executive director of CBE; Orville Sweeting of Yale University; and George Weber, associate director of CBE. Their comments were incisive and extremely useful. Even when I have failed to follow their advice, I have profited by weighing it. Whatever shortcomings remain in the book are obviously mine alone. I am also indebted to CBE for sponsoring this book and for administering a grant from the Old Dominion Foundation which allowed me to write it. Certain material from the book has appeared as articles in *The Saturday Review* and *The Times Educational Supplement* (London). These publications have kindly granted permission for the use of the material here in somewhat modified form.

J.D.K.

Who Controls American Education?

THE POWER OF THE FEDERAL GOVERNMENT

Chapter I

As MOST PEOPLE KNOW by now, the distribution of governmental power in the United States is undergoing some fundamental changes. On the one hand, the federal government is exercising much more authority over state and local government than ever before; on the other, there is much talk of decentralization and many efforts to make state and local government stronger than ever before. The result is called "Creative Federalism" by some and chaos by others.

In a series of actions over the last dozen years the federal government in all three branches has made clear its conviction that lower levels of government are unable, for whatever reasons, to cope with the civil rights movement and a number of other urgent problems. Most of these federal actions involve American education in one way or another. The central government has apparently decided that formal education is to be one of the chief instruments for solving all sorts of social and economic problems—poverty, hate, discrimination, unemployment, maladjustment, inequality. It has also decided that the states and local communities will have to be led, or if necessary coerced, by higher authority until they are willing and able to tackle these problems themselves. "The old system," as John W. Gardner, former Secretary of the Department of Health, Education, and Welfare, commented recently,

> of weak State and local government, minimum coordination, and casual communication among Federal, State, and local

levels is dying. Or to put the matter more bluntly, it's dead. We are busily constructing a new system and what it will look like when we get done no one knows.[1]

In this book I will neither endorse nor deprecate this redistribution of power, for my concern throughout is with educational, not party, politics. For better or for worse, the shifting governmental relationships that are so much a part of our public life today affect our educational system directly, and they are the right place for us to begin a consideration of who controls American education.

The Growing Authority of Congress

A glance at the historical record of Congress in educational legislation may help to put its flurry of recent activity into perspective. Congress has passed hundreds of pieces of educational legislation in its history, but the fundamental actions have been few. They are:

1. *The Land Ordinance of 1785.* Congress was worried in the 1780's about the orderly development of what was then the Northwest Territory. It adopted a series of ordinances affecting these lands and the way in which they were to be divided politically and physically. One of the stipulations of the 1785 ordinance was that one section out of each township (of thirty-six sections) was to be reserved for the establishment of public schools. By this simple device Congress established an early precedent for making its voice heard in education whenever it so desired.

2. *The Morrill Land Grant Act of 1862.* Named after a senator from Vermont, this act gave 30,000 acres of federal land to each state for each of its representatives in Congress, the purpose being to endow a college of agriculture and "mechanic arts." The government through this and succeeding legislation wound up giving 17,000,000 acres of land to the states who then sold most of it to finance the building and maintenance of "land grant" colleges. We now have sixty-eight such institutions, including a number of first-line universities such as Cornell, MIT, and the state universities

of Minnesota, Wisconsin, Illinois, and California. The far-reaching effects of this act are obvious.

3. *The Smith-Hughes Act of 1917.* This act was the first of a number of national vocational education acts. It grew out of World War I but was also a logical follow-up to the Morrill Act. It gave substantial aid to the states for training teachers of vocational subjects and for instruction in trades and home economics. With this and later acts (especially *The George-Barden Act of 1946*), Congress created a vast vocational education industry in American schools, the ramifications of which are felt throughout the school system, as well as in the halls of state legislatures (as we will have occasion to remark later in this book).

4. *The Servicemen's Readjustment Act of 1944.* This act, the "GI Bill of Rights," and similar ones for the Korean War and for Vietnam veterans, have had a momentous effect on American colleges and universities by financing the college education of millions of veterans. Since the first of the GI Bills, our institutions of higher education have never been the same.

5. *The National Defense Education Act of 1958.* After Sputnik I and II in the fall of 1957, Congress along with the rest of the country gave some serious attention to the quality of American education. One result was this act by which an unprecedented amount of money was given to the states and to colleges and universities to improve education in the sciences and foreign languages and for other purposes. It was enacted by Congress as a defense measure.

That brings the record down to the watershed of the 1960's, when a torrent of education bills have been debated in Congress. Between 1962 and 1967 alone, Congress passed perhaps thirty pieces of legislation which pumped a vast amount of federal money into the education and the occupational training of Americans. *The Manpower Development and Training Act of 1962; The Vocational Education Act of 1963; The Economic Opportunity Act of 1964; The Higher Education Act of 1965; The Elementary and Secondary Education Act of 1965;* plus the renewals, extensions, and expansions of these acts in 1966 and 1967: all this legislation comes to many billions of dollars and creates many new relationships between the federal government and the states and between both of them and the local education authorities.

Congress has never really worried much about what is alleged to be the constitutional prohibition against a federal role in education. Opponents of federal aid point out that the word "education" does not even occur in the Constitution and that all matters educational are therefore "reserved to the States" as provided in the Tenth Amendment. But Congress waves off this objection, as it does many others, merely by citing the "general welfare" clause of the Constitution which has always allowed it to legislate on questions for which specific constitutional authority does not exist.

It has been the same alleged inability or unwillingness of the states and cities to deal adequately with discrimination, pollution, urban renewal, medical care, mass transit, law enforcement, and a multitude of other problems, that has brought Congress into state and local affairs, just as Congress has now decided to come into education on a big scale. "Pragmatic accommodation where legal principle fails," as one political scientist puts it,[2] has been the characteristic of America's federal system from the beginning. So, good or bad, the role of Congress in American education is now great and certain to become greater. In other words the legislative branch for the first time in our history has assumed in the 1960's a major voice in American educational policy.

Education and the Judicial Branch

One could easily argue that the most powerful body now making educational policy in the United States is not Congress or the states or the local boards, but the Supreme Court. It would be hard to overstate the educational effects of a number of decisions of the "Warren Court," particularly the desegregation decision in 1954 (*Brown v. Board of Education of Topeka*) which struck down the doctrine of separate but equal educational facilities.

The Court's far-reaching decision in 1962 on the reapportionment of state legislatures (*Baker v. Carr*) and on congressional reapportionment in 1964 (*Wesberry v. Sanders*) could also ultimately have profound effects on education.

The American Supreme Court, passing as it does on the constitutionality not only of state and local laws but on acts of Congress and on actions of the executive branch, exercises a greater power than does the supreme court of any other country. But its power, like that of Congress and the President, has been felt in a really substantial way in education on only a few occasions and most of those in recent years (although many of its earlier decisions had educational implications). Now its decisions reach deeply into the traditional preserves of state and local educational authorities who find their freedom sharply curtailed. One may applaud or deplore this judicial control in American education, but it marks another big shift of power to the center.

Similarly the other federal courts now interpret the desegregation and related decisions of the Supreme Court in a wide variety of situations and often extend these decisions into new educational territory. A federal court in New York, for example, recently ruled (but was overturned on appeal) that children and parents have a *constitutional* right to be represented by an attorney at "guidance" hearings which may result in a student's suspension from school. Another federal court has granted a permanent injunction that requires a private college to accept qualified students without regard to color.

As I write, the most recent and surely the most spectacular exercise of power by a federal court in education is the lengthy opinion handed down in June 1967 by Judge J. Skelly Wright of the United States Court of Appeals for the District of Columbia. This opinion, which extended the desegregation decision into distant new ground, shocked and dismayed many people and delighted others. "Sociological jurisprudence," said *The New York Times,* no friend of segregated education. In effect, the judge declared *de facto* segregation not merely undesirable but unconstitutional. Further he declared that the well known "track" system of the Washington, D.C., schools, which was not very different from systems used in a great many schools in which different curriculums prevail for students of different abilities or desires, violated the constitutional rights of Negroes—as did optional school zones and the way in which the district authorities assigned teachers to schools.

If Judge Wright's opinion is upheld on appeal, the effects on American education could be even greater than those of the 1954 desegregation decision of the Supreme Court. The consequences for educational policy would be momentous in virtually every city in the country. Even if it is overturned the fact that such an opinion could come out of a federal court suggests how rapidly the central government is moving into the area of basic educational policy.

The United States Office of Education

The executive branch of the federal government is no less active than the other two. It not only carries out the mandates of Congress and the federal courts but undertakes many educational activities on its own initiative. The most important single executive agency is the Office of Education. Unlike other advanced countries, which are far more centralized politically than the United States, we have never had anything like a ministry of education. Almost all the national governments of Europe have a major division devoted to education, and this ministry has extensive powers over the nation's schools, their budgets, the training and licensing of teachers, standards and examinations, and general educational policy; and the head of the ministry usually sits in the cabinet. In France, Italy, Sweden, and other countries, the education ministry is by far the most important policy-making body in education.

Because of their political structure, other countries are also able to appoint national governmental commissions to investigate educational questions and make recommendations to which the government is expected to give serious consideration. Thus Britain's "Robbins Committee," for example, having made an exhaustive study a few years ago of higher education in England and having had its ambitious recommendations accepted by the government, became in effect a major policy-making body in English education. Such a committee would probably not be feasible in the United States and if feasible would not be very successful because of the absence of centralized authority able to do something about the committee's findings and recommendations. But this situation could change quickly, given the vaulting ambition of today's government agencies and the readiness of Congress to raise its voice in education.

The American government did not establish any agency at all in education until 1866 when Congress, after considerable debate, reluctantly created a Federal Department of Education for the purpose, as the act said,

> of collecting such statistics and facts as shall show the condition and progress of education in the several States and Territories, and of diffusing such information respecting the organization and management of schools and school systems and methods of teaching as shall aid the people of the United States in the establishment and maintenance of efficient school systems, and otherwise promote the cause of education throughout the country.

The new department got off to a dubious start under the mismanagement of an aging Henry Barnard. Congress was tempted to abolish it at the end of an unproductive first year but instead demoted it from a department to an "office."

For most of its first hundred years the Office of Education has been a minor cog in the governmental wheel and in the vast educational machinery of the country. Until the 1960's, most of the appointed commissioners of education were men of no particular ability or distinction and were, along with the office itself, creatures of the professional education establishment. The Office of Education has never performed its main job of gathering and disseminating educational statistics with efficiency or imagination; indeed it has much to answer for in failing to provide the country with current and reliable data that are indispensable to state and federal officials and to the educational field generally. Things are better now than in the recent past, but Office of Education statistics are still quite inferior to those of Britain, France, Germany, and many other countries that spend far less on the job.

The status of the Office of Education has changed dramatically since Sputnik. It has nearly tripled in size since that time and today is one of the most important agencies in Washington. No longer an obscure bureau that cab drivers can't find, the Office of Education now has plenty of "visibility," thanks to the exponential growth that has resulted from congressional appropriations which the office administers. It now commands the attention of Congress, and even more, of the states and cities. It is housed in a massive new building in sight of Capitol Hill and has nearly three thousand people administering over one hundred programs. Presumably it will soon have more space and more people running more programs.

What are these programs? They have been carved out of about twenty-five acts of Congress aimed at providing grants of money to selected schools, colleges, cities, states, school boards, and sundry agencies to finance in whole or in part such things as (1) construction of buildings or other educational facilities; (2) improvement of instruction or administration; (3) teacher-training programs and loans to prospective teachers; and (4) educational research.

These broad categories do not begin to suggest the scope and variety of Office of Education grants, which are now in the billions of dollars yearly and which encompass about every educational activity imaginable. Grants are made for buying educational television equipment, for example, or for studying ways of using it; for bringing foreign educators to the United States to observe our schools or sending ours abroad; for "desegregation training" of school personnel or improving the teaching of the handicapped; for helping the education of Cuban refugees or the occupational training of unemployed Americans; for providing graduate fellowships or undergraduate loans; for helping poets to write verse and photographers to take pictures. Just as cities and states have now taken to maintaining a liaison office in Washington, many city and state educational officials have come to the conclusion that it pays them to hire somebody just to keep abreast of Office of Education money for which they may be eligible.

The sudden growth of the Office of Education raises questions about the agency's influence on educational policy. Although Congress identifies the general purpose of the programs administered by the office, the detailed qualifications and guidelines that must be met by applicants for grants are established and enforced by the Office of Education itself. The discretion left to the administrators of the office is sometimes small, sometimes great. Either way, final judgments about who gets money and who does not are made by the office and therefore create some heated relationships between the office and those seeking its favors. The heat often reaches Congress, which in 1967 withdrew some of the powers of the office in dealing with states and cities and gave it instead directly to the states. The issue becomes particularly sticky when the Office of Education has a great many more applicants than funds and must therefore choose to support relatively few people and reject many, and when it seeks to carry out other congressional mandates such as Title VI of the 1964 Civil Rights Act forbidding federal money to anyone who practices discrimination.

Many of the troubles of the office, as well as the source of its influence over policy, comes from the fact that Congress has always insisted on appropriating money for "categorical" aid only, thereby raising cries and fears of "federal control of education." General, no-strings-attached aid to schools has been the goal of some members of Congress, including Senator Taft in 1948, and of many national groups for many years. But Congress to date remains unconvinced. It has always supplied federal money as an answer to specific problems: deprived childen, classroom shortages in higher education, teacher shortages, neglected subjects of the curriculum (especially when they are thought to relate to national defense), federally "impacted" areas, and unequal resources among the states. So far opposition from political and religious groups, the latter in particular, has blocked general aid. Nor has Congress itself been anxious to yield any of its power to lower levels of government. In view of the rapidly increasing involvement of Congress in education and of the increasing pressures for some kind of tax sharing plan between the federal government and the states, general aid to education will probably come in the future. Even so, it may have to come through the back door disguised as a means of achieving equality for all Americans or the protection of all children.

When general aid does come it will not displace, but will no doubt reduce, categorical aid. To the extent that it does, it will at least get the Office of Education out of the business of weighing proposals and judging applicants and thereby of influencing educational policy. Conceivably it might not work that way. If Congress were to insist on keeping track of how money for general aid was spent, it could wind up giving the Office of Education authority for enforcing some kind of minimum standards throughout the country. But the opposition of schoolmen to such a step would probably be massive. Both Congress and the office at the present time are wont to minimize the threat of federal control. They like to point out that the bulk of funds go for purposes defined not by the office but by a Congress that reflects the wishes of the public.

But the fact of control exists and must exist as long as grants are categorical. Willingly or not, the Office of Education for the first time in our history is a major policy-making force these days. It therefore finds itself in a recurring dilemma: it must make many choices and impose many criteria of its own creation at the same time that it must avoid any semblance of forcing its will on recipients. As a result the office, in my opinion and that of many others, is often in an untenable middle position that in effect defeats the "will of Congress."

This dilemma is neatly illustrated in the relationship of the Office of Education to the new "Regional Educational Laboratories," a relationship that is worth a bit of our time to examine. Title IV of the Elementary and Secondary Education Act of 1965 authorized the creation of a number of Regional Educational Laboratories that had been proposed in previous years by various advisory bodies. Their purpose was to increase the nation's investment in educational research and particularly in the dissemination of research findings and in educational reform generally. They were to be, that is, agencies comparable to industry's "research and development" organizations. They were to be under the control of distinguished people and were to bring an entirely new dimension into American education.

The idea of the regional labs owes a great deal to an agency called Educational Services Incorporated. ESI in turn grew out of MIT's well known Physical Science Study Committee. By way of reminder, PSSC was a program established in 1956 under the leadership of a number of outstanding physicists for the purpose of overhauling high school physics. It led to the establishment of ESI in 1958 as an administrative vehicle for the project. In succeeding years ESI organized and administered a number of other projects in curriculum reform and was the only organization of its kind and scope in the country. Among its distinguishing characteristics were two: it tackled the reform of basic academic subjects on a scale never before attempted; and in doing so it brought many kinds of people, especially recognized scholars and outstanding school teachers, into effective collaboration in a way never before done.

ESI people were active in the planning stages of the regional labs and helped push the proposal through Congress. It was the chance to multiply ESI and its pioneering development work that many people had in mind in supporting Title IV and the idea of a national network of regional labs. During congressional hearings on the 1965 Act, Francis Keppel, then Commissioner of Education, and John W. Gardner, as well as many scholars and scientists, testified enthusiastically on behalf of the idea of regional labs. They saw such labs as blue-ribbon agencies bringing many different sorts of people together—eminent scientists, hu-

manists, industrialists, authors, school teachers, and assorted intellectuals and professionals—to work at a job they had never
faced together before, that of educational reform. Gardner saw
the labs as organizations "combining the resources of MIT, IBM,
and the New York State Board of Regents." Here is the way that
President Johnson justified the creation of regional labs in his
Education Program Message to Congress in January 1965:

> Under the auspices of the National Science Foundation,
> educators have worked with scientists—including Nobel
> laureates—to develop courses which capture the excitement
> of contemporary science. They have prepared totally new
> instructional materials—laboratory equipment, textbooks,
> teachers' guides, films, supplementary reading, and examina-
> tions. After testing they are made available to public and
> private schools.
>
> We need to extend our research and development to his-
> tory, literature, and economics; to art and music; to reading,
> writing and spelling; to occupational, vocational, and tech-
> nical education. We need to extend it to all stages of learning
> —preschool, elementary and secondary schools, colleges and
> graduate training.
>
> Regional laboratories for education offer great promise.
> They draw equally upon educators and practitioners in all
> fields of learning—mathematicians, scientists, social scientists,
> linguists, musicians, artists, and writers.

Since Congress bought the regional labs on the basis of this
rather lofty vision, the Office of Education would seem to have
been given a pretty clear mandate as to the kind of agencies that
were supposed to be brought into being. But the Office of Education failed to carry out that mandate. As soon as the 1965 Act
passed, groups of people who call themselves professional educators began forming around the country to set up organizations
and qualify for all that federal money.

Let me digress long enough to say that the term "professional
educator" continues to mislead many people. Laymen naturally
assume that it encompasses anyone whose "profession" is "edu-

cation"—such as school teachers and college professors, and do not realize that the term is usually applied only to persons whose profession is in the formal study or administration of education, such as superintendents of schools, professors of education, officials of state departments of education, and administrators of professional associations. The term "educationist" or "educationalist," which is a perfectly good one in other countries, seems to be resented in the United States. Thus to keep the peace along with the ambiguity, I will use the term "professional educator" throughout the book.

Many of these new groups formed by professional educators were ultimately approved by the Office of Education and financed as regional laboratories, even though they bore little resemblance to the kind of agencies that were intended. We now have twenty such labs, none of which was modeled on ESI and all of which are under the strong domination of professional educators. The one exception is the lab in the New England area, Education Development Center, which escaped the pattern because it was itself a merger of ESI and another group. Unhappily the grand and glowing promise that Congress and others saw in the idea of the labs was proven false from the start. Neither the governing boards nor the staffs of the regional labs represent anything like the diversity of high-level talent envisioned by the planners. Nor do the research and development projects that the labs are now doing seem to be anything more than routine studies of a kind that have been done by professional educators for many years and that, in fact, the Office of Education has been financing under other programs.

The point of this sad tale is that the Office of Education, caught in the dilemma of trying to enforce the will of Congress and at the same time of trying to avoid the least suggestion of federal control, often takes a middle ground and fails to accomplish either end. If the office had taken a stronger line on the way in which the regional labs were to develop, as it obviously should have, the labs might indeed be one of the most promising developments in our educational history. Instead, they are, as one man close to them admits, "just another boondoggle"; or, as another said to me, "They are nothing but schools of education with lots of money and no students."

In other words a splendid and unique opportunity in the reform of American education was lost by the timidity of the Office of Education. Of course we must recognize that timidity was not the only problem. Professional educators, the principal benefactors of the regional labs, are themselves the dominant voice at the Office of Education. They have always controlled its administration and they have not been visibly disconsolate at seeing the regional labs become another well furnished wing on the professional clubhouse. But Congress, the taxpayers, and the schools are the losers.

Nor is the record of the office much better in the moneys it doles out in other programs. To take one such program for illustration, suppose we look at the Office of Education grants for educational research. For many years, especially the last decade during which the Cooperative Research Program has been in operation, the office has been a prime source of funds for research projects, the vast majority done by professional educators. In an examination of the record of the office in financing these projects, the words that come most often to one's mind are "trivia" and "duplication."

For example, the office over the last quarter of a century must have financed dozens of projects in the investigation of reading instruction in which professional educators whose views on reading instruction are well known and not varied do research on how to improve reading instruction. With what result? Is instruction in reading in American schools any better for these multiple studies? If so, the improvement is not discernible. Indeed one could say with justice that these studies, which begin with similar assumptions and come up with similar findings, merely contribute to the further entrenchment of a system of reading that has many manifest deficiencies. Another result, inevitably, is still more studies. The office recently announced, for example, a study of "Reading Readiness Tests as Predictors of Success in

Reading," which I have no hesitation in saying is at least the hundredth time that such a study has been made in the United States.

Consider the following research projects, which are but a dozen out of hundreds recently approved and financed by the Office of Education:

1. The Elementary School Principalship in Texas
2. The Motivational Patterns of Women Engaged in Educational Activities of Voluntary Organizations
3. Critical Reactions, Self-Concept, and Behavioral References
4. The Relation of Reading Achievement to One Aspect of "Realism" Among 7- to 12-Year-Old Boys
5. Nonovert Reinforced Cloze Procedure [sic]
6. Student and First-Year Teachers' Attitudes toward Self and Others
7. Relationship of Art Quality to Sociological, Motivational, and Economic Factors
8. Factors Affecting Learning to Read
9. Connotative and Associative Components of Creative Potential
10. Parental and Peer Group Pressures toward Deviant Student Behavior
11. Personality Factors and Their Influence on Clothing Fabric Selection by Delinquent Girls
12. The Organization of Educational Research in the United States

The last project piques one's curiosity since educational research in the United States could not be said to have any sort of organization. The recipients of grant No. 12 describe their project this way:

The chief technical problem of this study was to measure the numerous social conditions which might conceivably impinge on the production of research and of researchers by graduate schools of education. The techniques employed included (1) questionnaire surveys of education deans, research coordinators, directors of research units, project directors in units, and authors of published research reports, (2) field interviews and observations of selected research bureaus and centers and of the work of professional associations, (3) documentary analysis of materials solicited through questionnaires, (4) content analysis of school of education catalogs, research articles published in 1964, and research proposals submitted to the cooperative research program, U.S. Office of Education, and (5) secondary analysis of survey data from selected studies.

Perhaps the most charitable thing we can say about research of this sort is that it probably does not do any harm apart from consuming federal money. For years the administrators of the Office of Education have been selecting such projects out of many applications. What the rejected applications were like one can only imagine. One is free of course to believe in the urgency and significance of a study of "nonovert reinforced cloze procedure" or of the "connotative and associative components of creative potential," but others can surely be forgiven for feeling that the office's grant getters are, as Edith Wharton once remarked about another professional group, "in the thick of a lot of pretty thin things." If someone were to make a thorough survey of the research sponsored by the Office of Education over, say, the last twenty-five years, and in particular of the results achieved and the uses, if any, to which these results have been put, Congress might have a depressing surprise. A humorist might apply to the Office of Education to fund such a study.

Naturally money stimulates projects far more often than projects stimulate money, especially in education and especially where government funds are concerned. Some of our leading schools of education, for example, now have multimillion dollar budgets, over half of which are for government-sponsored research.

In moments of candor, some of our professional educators cheerfully acknowledge the waste in Office of Education programs, and are quite willing, at least in private, to admit that a quarter or a half of its research funds go to slovenly and unproductive projects. Whatever the true figure, the fact is that far more money is now available for things like educational research than there are or possibly ever can be first-rate researchers to spend it. The result is a lot of generated, opportunistic work that follows whatever research fads happen to be popular at any given time. One year the money is going into "creativity in learning," and people hastily put together projects to study this phenomenon; another year it might be "innovation in teaching"; currently the money is, as they say, "in poverty." A psychiatrist once asked Willie Sutton, the celebrated bank robber, why he robbed banks. "Because," said Sutton, "that's where the money is." A like motivation, I feel, is behind the bulk of federal educational research.

No doubt some good comes of all these programs, but whether it cancels out the bad is a moot point. By financing large numbers of inferior projects, the Office of Education might well have a highly negative influence on educational development and policy. Conversely, by failing to carry out the congressional will, it also has an effect on policy. Because it has large sums of money at its disposal and must choose the people who are to receive it, the office is necessarily a major force in shaping American education. The issue to be faced, therefore, is how to improve the quality of its influence.

Other Activities of the Executive Branch in Education

By no means is the involvement of the executive branch in education limited to programs of the Office of Education. The office spends somewhat less than half the federal funds spent on education, broadly considered. The rest is spent by agencies throughout the federal government whose programs, like those of the Office of Education, have grown haphazardly over the years.

In the Office of the President alone, we find such agencies as the Office of Economic Opportunity, the Office of Emergency Planning, the Office of Science and Technology, and the CIA, all sponsoring educational programs of some type. We find many so-called independent agencies, as diverse as the Atomic Energy Commission and the Appalachian Regional Commission or the

Smithsonian Institution, similarly engaged. Even the National Foundation on the Arts and the Humanities will be spending a sizable amount of money in the near future and exercising thereby an influence on education. Then there are the extensive educational programs, everything from fellowships to the running of schools, to be found in the major government departments— State, Defense, and the Department of Health, Education, and Welfare.

We find the Job Corps, Head Start, and VISTA at the Office of Economic Opportunity; we find the Neighborhood Youth Corps at the Department of Labor; we find the Cooperative Extension Service at the Department of Agriculture; we find NASA financing the development of curriculum materials for use in schools; we find the air force supporting doctorate study by civilians, the army supporting studies of human learning, the Department of State teaching history, economics, and foreign languages, and the Defense Department running a big school system. We find federal agencies financing specialized "not-for-profit" organizations like the Rand Corporation, MITRE, as well as university-affiliated research organizations such as MIT's Lincoln Laboratory or Johns Hopkins' Applied Physics Laboratory, all of which conduct educational programs. We even find the federal government operating what amounts to a center for graduate study in applied sciences at Oak Ridge—through the management of Union Carbide Company—to say nothing of the Atomic Energy Commission's educational programs at Los Alamos, Livermore, and numerous universities.

And of course we find the National Science Foundation, one of the most potent influences of all on American education in the postwar period. Since its inception in 1950, NSF has spent billions of dollars, currently about half a billion a year, on science and education. Much of this money goes to support curriculum reform, teacher training, and research projects of great diversity but directly related to schools and colleges. In teacher training alone NSF has been a major maker of policy through its many hundreds of "in-service institutes," into which have gone hun-

dreds of millions of dollars, for teachers of science and mathematics. One need not be able to trace this influence with precision
to say that NSF has been and continues to be one of the main
channels through which the power of the federal government is
felt over education.

All told the federal government will spend over twelve billion
dollars on educational programs in 1968, of which 46 percent
will be spent by the Department of Health, Education, and
Welfare—a growth of over 27 percent for HEW in two years.[3]
If the country is now spending nearly fifty-five billion dollars a
year on all of education, or about 7 percent of our Gross National
Product, and that seems to be the statisticians' best guess, the
federal government's share is somewhere between 15 and 25 percent of the nation's education bill, depending on what one
chooses to include in the term "education." Its share of the national bill for public elementary and secondary education is
about 9 percent. From any point of view this is a substantial
federal role and one that has grown very rapidly. In higher education, the federal government is now the largest single source
of tax moneys, supplying more funds than all the states put together for their institutions.

Not all federal power is tied to money. Indirect influence on
educational policy is exerted in many ways. When the President
calls a White House Conference on Education, for instance, he
is using the moral authority of the government to affect educational decisions. When Congress directs that a comprehensive
study be made that relates closely to education, as it did in the
case of the 1966 Coleman Report (*Equality of Educational Opportunity*), it too affects the decisions made by a great many educational officials. When the Commission on Civil Rights issues
such reports as "Racial Isolation in the Public Scrools," "A Time
to Listen . . . A Time to Act," and "Education Parks" (all in
1967), it seeks to influence educational policy, as did the Special Advisory Commission on Civil Disorders appointed at the
height of the summer riots in 1967. When the President's Commission on Law Enforcement and Administration of Justice re-

ports as it did in 1967, recommending major changes in teacher licensing practices, in textbooks, and in teaching methods, it brings the federal government rather directly into educational policy.

For that matter, one could make a case for the power of a body like the President's Science Advisory Committee, which indeed has affected American educational policy in many significant ways. One even finds the power of the federal government exercised by representatives of the Department of Defense, who in 1967 condemned the University of Michigan (a major recipient of Defense contracts) as a school for "rich white students" and who recommended that the university adopt new hiring practices for secretarial and janitorial help and establish new admissions policies for students that would allow more Negroes to enter whether they met the usual standards or not.

I don't mean to suggest in all this that federal power in education should be diminished, though that might be a worthy long-term goal. I do not myself share the fears so often voiced by schoolmen and others about federal control or federal "dictatorship" in education. I find it hard to take seriously a comment like the following, typical of the attitude of many professional educators:

> The government cannot continue to make inroads on the professional function of the school in such vital matters as planning and evaluation without eventually undermining the school's will and capacity to make its own major decisions on what it needs and how to proceed. Already there are schools which have shelved their own plans in haste to submit proposals more conformative to government stipulations, and others with frustrated officials whose high-priority projects, under existing provisions, cannot qualify for Federal assistance.[4]

My impression is that most schoolmen, far from being rich with "high-priority" projects of their own and being frustrated by federal stipulations, are exceedingly eager to dip into the pork barrel and quite willing to create any sort of program that will let them. Oddly enough, the same people who denounce federal power today are often those who yesterday were telling us how inadequate and obsolete was the whole idea of local control of education and how important it was to centralize authority so as to get things done.

I feel that federal power in education with all the attendant waste and inefficiency may be better at the moment than the waste and inefficiency of the states, which I will discuss in Chapter IV. Our long-term goal might be to improve the educational policy-making capacities of the states so as to eliminate or minimize the federal role; that indeed is a goal supported by many people in Congress and some in the Office of Education. Meanwhile, we might improve the educational operations of the federal government as well. We could begin by recognizing the power that has accrued to the federal government in recent years and insisting that this power be exercised overtly rather than covertly. We could also put an end to the hodgepodge of multiple and overlapping federal programs in education and insist on some measure of coordination and "rationalization"; the savings would be large even though the risk of standardization and rigidity would also grow.

Finally, the Office of Education could be made less lopsided in its administrative staff, making room for more teachers and scholars and fewer professional educators, thus achieving a staff more representative than the present one of the educational community at large. Francis Keppel during his tenure as Commissioner of Education did a great deal to reorganize the office and to raise its intellectual sights. He brought in a number of good people (many of whom have since left) to represent the academic subjects, and he did not hesitate to step on the toes of the old guard when it was necessary. But the office is still strongly dominated by professional educators who still dole out great sums of money according to their own priorities and prejudices. To change the priorities and prejudices, one must change the people.

The internal reforms started by Keppel should be kept moving, and no better time can be found for it than during a period of explosive growth like the present.

The federal role in education, however the quarrel between categorical and general aid is ultimately settled, is going to keep going sharply up. Keppel's comment that the government's role is rather like that of a "junior partner" to the states and local school authorities may have been true not many years ago, but it is true no longer. "From now on," as one political scientist observes at the end of a study of the Office of Education,

> the problem for Presidents, faced with the costs of international conflict and the dangers of domestic inflation, will be less to induce congressional support for education than to keep congressional action within fiscal and budgetary bounds. . . . At some critical point, what starts as presidential initiative becomes a self-generating congressional force. This happened long ago in the fields of health research and related health services. There are many who feel that this has already happened in key areas of defense hardware and federal paybills. It has most certainly happened in education.[5]

It most certainly has, though the general public may not yet have noticed the fact. The sooner it does, the better, for the power of the federal government is now perhaps the most important element of all the kaleidoscope of our educational politics.

THE INFLUENCE
OF TEACHERS
ORGANIZATIONS

Chapter II

ONE OF THE MOST SURPRISING PHENOMENA of the 1960's has been the raucous rise of classroom teachers and their professional organizations, a rise that owes something to the fact that teachers have had a sellers' market for their services but also to the civil rights movement and the concentration of national attention on the inner cities. Even when teachers as a group were notable for their apathy and lack of influence over educational policy, they were still a power to be reckoned with; they were one of the largest organized groups in the country and were often represented on the national scene by powerful administrative groups that claimed to speak for them. Now teachers are losing their traditional fears. They are beginning to speak for themselves and to make loud demands. They and their professional organizations promise to be a much more significant force in the future than in the past, and I therefore propose to discuss their organizations in this chapter, reserving for Chapter III a consideration of other national agencies and groups.

Before looking at the two main teachers organizations in the country, the National Education Association and the American Federation of Teachers, let me record a few basic facts that we need to keep in mind about the size and makeup of the teaching force in the United States:

In 1967 there were 2,100,000 school teachers in the country
  90 percent of them were in the public schools, the rest in private, mostly Roman Catholic, institutions
60 percent of them were elementary school teachers

69 percent of them were female

93 percent of them held at least a bachelor's degree in education or some other subject

24 percent of them held the master's degree in education or some other subject

65 percent of them had been teaching for less than ten years

Their average age was 36

Their average salary was $7,000, slightly higher for secondary school teachers, slightly lower for elementary

There was one teacher for every 27 students in the elementary schools

There was one teacher for every 21.4 students in the secondary schools.

The figures are approximate and, of course, change slightly from year to year, but they at least give us a quick profile of the nation's teaching force.

The Structure of the NEA and the AFT

The NEA and the AFT are quite unequal in size and assuredly in outlook, but I will discuss them together because they are the only teachers organizations of national significance. In higher education there are also teachers organizations, such as the American Association of University Professors, but their national influence is not large. Of our public school teachers, nine out of ten belong to some kind of local or state professional group, though a great many do not belong to either of the national organizations.

The NEA is older by a few years than the United States Office of Education, having been established in Philadelphia by a handful of schoolmen in 1857. Today the NEA has over a million members, having grown explosively in the last few decades (its membership in 1918 was only 10,100). Its membership increases, though not its percentage of the nation's teachers, as education and the teaching force expand. For a number of years its membership has remained at about 52 percent of our public school teachers, not an impressive proportion in view of the age and affluence of the organization. The NEA calls itself "the largest professional organization in the world," which may well be right; but when it also claims to be the "only overall professional association for teachers in the United States," it is merely playing with words.

Over the years the NEA has developed an elaborate bureaucracy and hierarchy. Theoretically its main policy-making body is the "Representative Assembly," consisting of over 7,000 members! Actually policy is made most of the time by the executive staff of the organization with the concurrence of a board of directors of 92 members and an executive committee of 11. All of the states have statewide teachers associations that are affiliated with, and pay dues to, the NEA. These affiliates are frequently large organizations in themselves and powerful lobbies in state legislatures. In addition, almost all school systems of any size in the United States have some kind of local teachers organizations. Local groups are often large and powerful bodies also; no fewer than 8,501 of these local associations are dues-paying affiliates of the NEA, their dues being filtered through state affiliates.

But the NEA is much more than a giant structure of state and local affiliates. It is also—indeed it is mainly—a convoluted collection of over seventy-five "Departments," "Divisions," "Commissions," and "Committees," all living happily together in a new building in downtown Washington. Separate professional organizations within the NEA exist for school principals to join (one for elementary school principals and another for secondary), for superintendents of schools, for teachers of math or home economics or physical education or speech or sundry other subjects. Divisions exist for research, for public relations, for lobbying ("Federal Relations"), and for a galaxy of other activities. There are separate groups concerned with professional ethics, school safety, civil rights, and the American Legion. There are even groups, such as the Council of Chief State School Officers, that are not formally affiliated with the NEA and that claim to be independent of it, but that are housed rent-free at the NEA headquarters.

To support this labyrinthine structure, the NEA has a budget many times the size of other professional organizations in the United States or abroad. I have never seen the true scope of the NEA budget cited in public. It is a tricky document to examine and one gets only grudging, not to say devious, help at NEA headquarters in analyzing it. Most journalists and commentators simply multiply the standard membership dues by the number of NEA members and come up with the budget. Thus if the NEA has a million members, they reason, and charges them $10.00 a year for dues, it has a budget of $10,000,000, not a paltry sum. However, the NEA's true income is much more various. Dues, for example, come in several forms and are calculated differently in different documents. The NEA customarily reports to its membership an income from dues a good deal lower than what it reports to the Internal Revenue Service. It reports to its membership an income of perhaps $200,000 a year from the sale of its publications, but reports to IRS an income from publications well over $2,000,000.

No doubt the differences are attributable to accounting practices, but they make it difficult for one to pin down the financial facts, such as the fact that the NEA's income is more than double that derived from basic membership dues. Its income beyond basic memberships is derived from the additional dues that people must pay in order to belong to one or more of those specialized professional departments of the NEA. These departments produce at least another $10,000,000 a year (members of the physical education department alone pay in another $2,000,-000 in dues). Substantial income is also realized from advertising, from convention exhibits, from educational tours, from investments, from grants and gifts, and from special contributions. All told, I would estimate the NEA's budget at something over $25,-000,000 a year. Moreover, since the NEA raised its dues in 1967, effective 1968, to $15.00 for a basic membership, its total income now is presumably well over $30,000,000 a year. Such an income makes the NEA the wealthiest professional organization in the country, if not in the world.

The AFT plays David to the NEA Goliath. It is much younger, having been founded in 1916 as a part of the labor union movement, and is now an affiliate of the AFL-CIO. It is much smaller and poorer, with a membership in 1967 of about 140,000, which itself represents an explosive growth in the 1960's concentrated in big northern cities. Membership is generally restricted to classroom teachers and to assistant principals or other administrators who do not have direct authority over teachers. Like the NEA, the AFT has local affiliates, about six hundred, and these local groups of teachers compete, of course, with local NEA groups. It also has state affiliates, though fewer than the NEA and much less developed. Its headquarters' budget is probably about $2,000-000 a year, met by dues and by gifts from other unions. The administrative structure is far simpler than that of the NEA and gives members a more direct voice in the work of the organization.

Ideologically the NEA and the AFT are a kind of two-party system in education, however unequal they may be in size and resources. They find it possible to take common ground on a few matters, and have even toyed once or twice with the idea of merging, but most of the time they emphasize rather than conceal their differences; they are, after all, in strenuous competition for the allegiance and dues of teachers.

Even a cursory visit to the headquarters of each organization points up some of these differences. The NEA is housed in shiny new headquarters within sight of the White House, in a very large building of marble and tinted glass similar to the functional but unlovely egg-crate office buildings that deface much of downtown Washington and other cities. Any layman visiting its multitudinous offices and talking with a typical selection of its administrators would come away with an impression of, to use a Hemingway phrase, a clean, well lighted place. Orderliness, respectability, affluence, officiousness, caution, efficiency of a sort, and an unadventuresome dullness are its most evident surface characteristics. The staff has long since grown accustomed to the comfortable solvency of the organization and to executive salaries ($50,000 for the executive secretary) that one does not find in crusading agencies or those with a sense of some kind of mission.

A visit to the AFT headquarters in Chicago is a different experience. Housed until mid-1967 in a cramped, run-down edifice in Rush Street, in sight of assorted girlie shows and tourist traps, the AFT gives one an impression of exactly what it is: a peppery, irreverent, disorganized, free-wheeling bunch of amateurs. Its administrators often exhibit an old-fashioned labor-union aggressiveness, dedication to a cause, suspiciousness of "management" in all its forms, and a dislike of the NEA that is only matched by the NEA's dislike of it. With power, however, is coming greater sophistication. The AFT, recognizing its need to exert some national as well as local influence, moved its offices in the summer of 1967 to Washington, D.C., not too far from the NEA Goliath and is beginning to conduct its affairs in a more professional fashion than in the past.

In both places one encounters a certain uneasiness at having writers and journalists around, and a marked lack of candor on such subjects as memberships, budgets, lobbying activities, and internal operations. Full disclosure is not one of the virtues of either organization, though both are quite willing to fill a visitor's ears with horrendous tales about the other.

Both organizations fill the usual functions of professional associations. They organize conferences by the dozen, conduct studies, publish books and magazines and newsletters with abandon, investigate grievances of their members against employers, sponsor speakers, lobby along the corridors of power in Washington, and promote the general welfare of teachers and, in the NEA's case, of administrators. All this sounds routine enough but is far from being so.

NEA and AFT Policies

An agonizing reappraisal is now going forward at the good gray NEA, which in the past has been the heart of the "establishment." I should like to pause for a moment over this somewhat derogatory term, which appears often in this book and in the general press these days. The term "establishment" was first applied in this way to American education, I believe, by me in a book on teacher training that appeared in April 1963. I was glad to see the term picked up and popularized, for it is a useful bit of shorthand. It seems now to have come into pretty general use but naturally runs the risk of taking on different meanings, depending on who uses it. I continue to use the term "establishment" simply as a means of referring to the congeries of associations, agencies, and groups that, taken together, pretty well control, so it seems to me, the enormous and lucrative enterprise of teacher education in the United States and that also exert a strong, often controlling, influence over the administration of schools and many other aspects of American education. I encompass within the word such organizations as the NEA and its many subgroups (especially its administrative groups), state departments of education, departments and schools of education in our colleges and universities, educational accrediting organizations, and various other groups made up entirely of, or dominated by, professional educators. These persons, I feel, share a similar kind of educational background themselves and tend to take the same approach to most educational problems. Their organizations usually support and reinforce one another's policies.

These homogeneous organizations and like-minded people represent only one segment of the American educational community, not to mention the general public. I believe that they have managed to accumulate over the years a dangerous degree of control over education and to disfranchise not only classroom teachers but academic scholars and the body politic. I do not suggest that they are a sinister phenomenon or that these folk sit around dimly lit, smoke-filled rooms at the NEA plotting to subvert the country. Their remarkable success in vaulting themselves into the educational catbird seat owes as much to the apathy of the rest of us as to their own power politics. Nor do I mean to lump all professional educators together into some kind of indiscriminate mass, ignoring the obvious fact that their ranks exhibit some variety and individualism—though not nearly as much as one might assume, given their numbers.

I am only saying that professional solidarity, a lack of strong intellectual inquiry, an absence of internal criticism, an intolerance of outside criticism, and a perfectly ordinary yen for empire building, are all characteristics of American professional educators. It was not always so. Conventions of the NEA, for example, in the early part of this century were often lively forums for debate and internal criticism. But today professional educators, acting through their various professional agencies, are probably the most powerful bloc, albeit a special-interest bloc, in American education. They do indeed constitute an establishment. People say there is a new establishment now forming and displacing the old, a view I do not entirely share and one to which I will return in the last chapter.

Because the NEA embraces not only classroom teachers but also school principals, superintendents, professors of education, and educational administrators in general, and because it has always had much more money than any other agency, it has been the main voice of the establishment in the past. Mostly it has been a conservative, stand-pat force with a big stake in maintaining the educational status quo. It has resisted any but the most innocuous criticisms of American education, and its various departments and divisions have often sought by fair means or foul to gag those who have dissented from establishment dogma. It has rarely used its wealth to sponsor anything more than pale and administratively attractive improvements in educational policies and practice. I cannot recall any proposal or program of the NEA that anyone could regard as radical.

For many years the NEA has been one of the principal lobbies on Capitol Hill, but curiously one of the least effective. As a tax-exempt agency, it is supposed to devote "no substantial part of its activities" to trying to influence legislation. In fact, it spends a lot of money in this fashion, though under the guise of "informational reports" or by answering congressional "requests." How much it actually spends is a question that could only be answered by a kind of fiscal analysis that has never been made at the NEA. On rare occasions the NEA can make its weight felt in Congress, as when it opposes bills that give federal money to private educational establishments; but on the whole its legislative accomplishments have been remarkably meager. If the AMA had got no more results from its lobbying expenditures over the years than has the NEA, the membership would presumably demand some changes.

Not so with the state affiliates of the NEA, a subject that I will discuss in Chapter IV. State teachers association are a powerful force in many a state legislature, sometimes the most powerful of all. A few years ago three political scientists made an intensive study of the educational politics of three states (Illinois, Michigan, and Missouri) and found that "In each state surveyed, legislators frequently singled out the education interests [chiefly the NEA state affiliate] as the most powerful in the state." [1] The same conclusion has been reached in a number of other single-state studies and only reinforces what has been widely acknowledged for years. NEA state affiliates are one of the largest organized groups in the states and usually have their headquarters in the capital city, where their officials spend a good deal of time dealing with state politicians. The AFT, however, has much less leverage in the state legislatures, and its state federations are not yet an important part of the AFT's structure. They can bring some pressure to bear on state legislators from urban, Democratic constituencies, but their power in general is only a shadow of the NEA's.

Both groups produce a flood of publications, a primary means, they assume, of making their influence felt. The NEA's innumerable publications are handsomely turned out, sometimes in a slick public-relations manner with lots of colorful but meaningless illustrations, and often on expensive coated paper. In substance its publications stretch from the uniquely useful, as in its statistical compilations, to the incredibly bad, as in *The NEA Journal*. The bad ones are rather more frequent, and the *Journal* is representative of them. It goes automatically to members and therefore enjoys the greatest circulation and probably the greatest advertising revenue of any professional journal in the country. Its influence, however, is nonexistent, and its readership, one suspects, is vastly lower than its circulation. In content it is the sort of fare that Nicholas Murray Butler must have had in mind when he observed that "educational literature is not nutritious as a steady diet." The *Journal* is not so much anti-intellectual as nonintellectual. Its pages are devoted to sophomoric pieces on current events in education, inspirational notes for teachers, and simple NEA propaganda. No one would accuse it of trafficking in unorthodox or challenging ideas. It is, in a word, the image of its master, but one hopes that it is not also the image of the American teacher.

Other NEA publications, such as the pronouncements of the Educational Policies Commission (an establishment-dominated body to be dissolved in 1968 after thirty years of NEA-financed operation), or the yearbooks of the various departments, are simply establishment documents that reinforce NEA positions. The AFT's publications are at least a refreshing change from the blandness of the NEA. They too have a party line to promote but are less rigid and more lively and are not afraid of unorthodox ideas. Although the AFT's publications are cheaply produced and unattractive to the eye, they will tell a layman more about the important things happening in education than most NEA publications.

Over the last few years the NEA has been seriously jolted and its influence threatened. Its role as boss of the establishment has been challenged by a change, if not a transformation, in the United States Office of Education, by the success of notable reform groups who have created the "new curricula," and by various kinds of fallout from the civil rights bomb. The monopoly that the NEA has long enjoyed as the only national teachers organization of real significance has been broken by the militant AFT. As late as the Eisenhower Administration it was said that the Office of Education was only a lily in the NEA pond and that Office of Education people from the commissioner on down regularly phoned the NEA before making important decisions. Thus no eyebrows were raised when Lawrence G. Derthick, Commissioner of Education in the Eisenhower years, resigned to move into a high-paying job at the NEA. In the same period, they say, Arthur S. Flemming, Secretary of the Department of Health, Education, and Welfare, took to phoning the NEA from his limousine to keep the establishment abreast of the progress of educational legislation.

Beginning with Kennedy's appointment of Sterling M. McMurrin as commissioner, the tradition of drawing commissioners from establishment ranks only and with the blessing of the NEA was broken. And with the regime of McMurrin's successor, Francis Keppel, who rammed through a major reorganization of the Office of Education, the end of an era of NEA domination probably began. The Office of Education is still a long way from what it might be, but it at least is something more than a captive agency now.

Even more traumatic for the NEA have been the recent, dramatic gains of the AFT. The 1960's have seen a series of strident contests in the northern cities between an overweight, slow-footed NEA and a lean and hungry AFT—contests in which local teachers have voted for the organization they wanted to represent them as bargaining agent with the local school board. Beginning in 1961 with a victory as convincing as it was surprising in one of the most important constituencies in the country, New York City, the AFT has gone on to further victories in such major northern cities as Chicago, Detroit, Cleveland, and Philadelphia. In 1967 the AFT also won Washington, D.C., and Baltimore and seems to have every chance of extending its string of successes through the decade.

To appreciate the effect of these victories on the NEA, one might imagine the reaction of the AMA if an upstart group of physicians plumping for socialized medicine won the allegiance of a majority of their fellow physicians in half a dozen of our largest cities. The AMA would scarcely have a choice as to whether to stick to the old policies. Neither does the NEA have a choice. It must either adopt AFT policies and tactics or counter them with something new of its own. It has chosen to try a bit of both.

What are the AFT policies that have been so effective? Chiefly its militancy—which means its willingness to resort to labor's big stick, the strike and the threat of a strike. Strikes by teachers and other public employees are usually unlawful, but the AFT does not openly advocate such strikes; it prefers to accent the positive and to speak of collective bargaining as its main concern and of the improvement of education through the improvement of teaching conditions. But in fact a number of AFT strikes have taken place successfully, so far with only two instances of punitive action by the courts, one a minor incident in Newark, New Jersey, and the other a token fine and imprisonment against the New York City AFT local and its president. That local is the United Federation of Teachers with fifty thousand members. It is one of the largest and most aggressive union locals in the nation and makes up fully a third of the entire AFT membership.

It was also in the fall of 1967 that the nation really became conscious of the growing power of teachers. Strikes and threats of strikes in a number of large cities besides New York brought teachers organizations for the first time to the sustained attention of the mass media. In an atmosphere of accusation and recrimination between teachers and politicians, and often between teachers who defied legal prohibitions and professional educators who deplored the "lesson" in lawbreaking they were setting their students, the teachers usually won. There seems every prospect that they will go on winning in the future.

Traditionally the NEA has denigrated strikes by teachers and still denigrates teachers unions. It has always talked about the "professionalism" of teachers and the need for grievance procedures, but has consistently denounced any use of the AFT's final weapon. However, after the AFT's big win in New York City in 1961, the NEA was forced into a new policy. It came up with something called "sanctions" which in their effects are hard to distinguish from strikes. By 1967 the NEA had invoked sanctions three times against entire states: Utah in 1964 where it won concessions; Oklahoma in 1965 where it also won concessions; and Florida in 1967 and 1968 where it was much less successful but where the final result is not yet clear. Sanctions have been invoked also against a number of individual school systems of small and medium size, and in 1967 against one large city, Baltimore.

Sanctions are simply a form of boycott. When the NEA resorts to them it urges the nation's teachers to boycott jobs in the sanctioned area and threatens them if they take such a job; the threat is in telling them that they may be violating the NEA Code of Ethics if they fail to respect the sanctions. It also urges national industries not to open new plants or conduct other new business in the area.

Applied in this way sanctions seem no different from the secondary boycott with which the NEA likes to charge the AFT in the case of the Kingsport Press. When some of the printing trades struck the Kingsport Press, a large textbook manufacturer, in 1963 (a case that was still unsettled in 1967), the AFT brought pressure to bear on some school boards with which it was the bargaining agent to boycott books from the Kingsport Press. The AFT's role in this case is certainly a suspect one at best, but no more reprehensible, it seems to me, than the NEA's sanctions that seek an industrial boycott of a whole state.

In a word, there is no practical difference between the AFT's strikes and the NEA's sanctions except the euphemisms adopted by both groups. The NEA at its annual convention in 1967 felt so threatened by the AFT's success as to make a historic turnabout and decide to support "work stoppages" by its locals, or "mass resignations" or "withdrawals of service" or other actions that may parade under labels but that mean strikes.

So rapidly has the movement grown toward "collective negotiations" (another euphemism: for "negotiations" read "bargaining") whether of the NEA or the AFT variety, that a dozen states now have legislation that extends bargaining rights to government employees in general and to teachers in particular. In 1960 only 5 percent of American teachers were so covered. Now it may be as high as 30 percent. It may soon be a majority. The next step will probably be a drive on the part of the AFT and possibly the NEA to legitimatize teacher strikes through state legislation.

Other differences between the two teachers organizations are important but may be diminished or erased in the future, as has pretty well been the case with their attitude toward strikes. For example, the NEA has always campaigned for a "unified profession" by which it meant membership in a single, monolithic association of all teachers, administrators, and other kinds of school personnel. This policy has inevitably meant that the administrator groups within the NEA, such as the American Association of School Administrators, have dominated the organization. Administrators have always been in a stout majority on both the board of directors and the board of trustees of the NEA, even though they have always been numerically a small minority of the NEA membership. The NEA staff too has been heavy with administrative types and light on classroom teachers. To put it bluntly, the professional educator for years has disfranchised the teacher in the teacher's own organization, and the voice of the NEA has therefore been the voice of the establishment.

Among the many deleterious effects of the NEA's being run, not by teachers but by teachers' bosses, is a habit school administrators have of pressuring their teachers to join. Ask any school principal or superintendent if he forces his teachers to join the NEA and he will deny it, probably with indignation. Ask teachers and you will often get a different response. Nobody knows what the NEA's membership would be if it were truly voluntary, but it would be a good deal smaller than it is.

Coercion can be subtle or ham-fisted, depending on the administrator. One administrator may simply decree that teachers' dues will be deducted from paychecks, another may persuade recalcitrant teachers to join the NEA by giving them the dirty jobs until they see the light (one even kept a teacher after school to do janitorial work until he joined up), another may just have a cozy off-the-record chat "for the teacher's own good"— after all, membership in the NEA bespeaks a "professional attitude" on the part of the teacher. Usually the teacher gets the message and sends in his application.

The AFT naturally likes to stress the coercive membership habits encouraged by the NEA, and frequently tries to collect statewide evidence of it, as it did recently in Minnesota, Colorado, and Wisconsin. But it finds such evidence hard to pin down; or rather, it finds plenty of evidence but can find few teachers willing to testify in court against their administrators. My own sympathies are with the AFT in this matter and I wish them success, for the arm-twisting proclivity of school administrators in the interests of the professional organization that they themselves dominate has long been one of the more unsavory aspects of the NEA. But I must say too that the AFT might not be any more enlightened itself if it reversed roles with the NEA. Two investigators concluded in 1966, after reviewing the available evidence, that administrators do indeed exercise compulsion over teachers and do indeed force them to join the NEA. They also concluded that the AFT was not wholly innocent of the same practice, only much more limited in opportunity.[2]

An organization like the NEA does not exist in other countries. Throughout Europe teachers and administrators belong to separate associations in recognition of their different and often conflicting interests. In England, for example, the main organization for teachers in primary and nonselective secondary schools is the National Union of Teachers, which bars administrators; it is probably the largest teachers organization in Europe and is predominantly female. Teachers in the selective secondary schools of England belong to another organization, just as they do in most other countries. Throughout Europe, that is, teachers from the selective secondary schools prefer to belong to their own high-prestige professional organizations. In some countries these organizations are a major influence on educational policy. France's *Association des Agrégés,* for example, to which belong those teachers who have passed the national, fiercely competitive *agrégation,* is one of the most powerful bodies in French education.

We lack any such group in the United States with which our best teachers could exercise a greater voice in policy than they now do through any professional organization. Various attempts have been made in the past to create a senior, prestige association, but none has had much success. Currently the Society of Academic Teachers, which was organized in suburban Philadelphia in 1964, is making another such attempt. It requires members to have not only a master's degree in their teaching field but a record of demonstrated superiority in teaching. This society may have more chance of success than previous organizations if it can convince the best of our teachers that they would be better off in their own professional association than in either the NEA or the AFT. I hope it can, but doubt that it will be able to counter the power of the other two groups sufficiently to become a significant force.

Likewise, school administrators in England and Europe belong to their own associations, and often have separate groups for male and female administrators. Then there are many other teachers groups with special appeals. In England, for instance, there is the National Association of Schoolmasters, which restricts its members to men teachers and campaigns for higher salaries for men. The same kind of diversification prevails in other countries, sometimes with a dozen different organizations competing for the allegiance of teachers, but never with one like the NEA.

Thus the AFT's taunt to the NEA that it is only a "company union" is not wide of the mark. In response to the AFT's policy of barring administrators, the NEA has moved in recent years to give the bulk of its membership (that is, teachers) a larger voice in policy. It has added teachers to various policy-making bodies and has generously financed its new Urban Services Division, which is concerned mostly with teacher welfare. In 1967 the Michigan Association of School Administrators, an NEA affiliate, took the unprecedented step of withdrawing from the NEA on the grounds that a school administrator could not justify a dual role: first, that of acting as the school board's executive officer and often as its chief negotiator in bargaining talks with teachers, and second, that of a member along with the same teachers of the same professional organization with which he might be bargaining. If more teachers and administrators became sensitive to the contradiction of their belonging to the same organization, we might see a genuine reconstruction of the NEA in the future, particularly if, as seems certain, teachers become steadily more militant.

The NEA and AFT differ on still other policies. The NEA has been exceedingly slow to adopt a policy against segregated local and state affiliates, which prevail in the South. For years the NEA ignored the problem, then put a smoke screen over it, and finally in 1967 adopted a resolution requiring integration of state and local affiliates by 1970. Having taken action so belatedly, the NEA is now confronted with the very real possibility that disaffected Negro teachers will organize their own professional association to compete with both the NEA and AFT. The obvious reason for the NEA's lack of deliberate speed in desegregating its affiliates was the fear of losing members, but its tardiness does no credit to an organization that talks as much as does the NEA about democracy, ethics, and "teacher rights and responsibilities."

The AFT for its part has had a policy since 1951 of refusing to charter new locals that practice discrimination, and a policy against segregation in existing locals since the Supreme Court's 1954 decision about separate but equal schools. As a result of these policies, the AFT lost its chapter in Atlanta and other southern cities in the 1950's. Over seven thousand members disaffiliated, a serious loss for a small organization. So again the two groups have now moved closer together than they have been at any time in the past, largely because of pressures brought to bear on the NEA by the AFT.

The growth of collective bargaining in American school systems, and the acceptance of bargaining by school boards and administrators, is one of the most notable developments in education since World War II. It seems clear that bargaining between local boards and NEA and AFT locals will continue to grow at an accelerating pace. Teachers have already started to bargain in many areas for a great deal more than salaries, as has been true of industrial unions for a long time. Teachers are increasingly demanding a voice in general school policy—in textbook selection, in curriculum development, in conditions of work (such as size of classes, use of teacher aides, hours of work), and even in such matters as the appointment of department heads and other school administrators. In other words, all things will be negotiable in the future that any given school board is willing to negotiate or can be made to negotiate. It is not at all difficult to foresee a time when virtually all American teachers will be employed under collective bargaining contracts that cover not only salaries but a long list of other items.

The political ramifications are obviously great. Teachers will exercise more control in the immediate future than they ever have in the past over educational policy. Not long ago American teachers were distinguished by their lack of influence and their apparent lethargy or helplessness in matters of basic policy. I and many other people deplored this willingness of teachers to yield to administrators many of the functions they themselves might fill more effectively. Now, however, one can easily imagine a dangerous reversal in the power of teachers, especially if the NEA and AFT are able to compose their differences so well that a marriage of the organizations takes place. If the major policies of these two national groups continue to converge, the groups may themselves merge. Even now, the only real obstacles to merger lie in the union affiliation of the AFT and the position of administrators in the NEA. The latter problem may be soluble but the former is difficult. For a merger to take place the NEA would have to abandon its independent stance and join the ranks of labor, or the AFT would have to abandon its union ties and join the NEA to make a new independent organization. Either move is possible but not probable in the immediate future.

If a merger is effected in the future, I, for one, look with unease on the possible consequences, especially if, as has been suggested from time to time, an even larger merger is effected with such groups as the American Association of University Professors. A single, monolithic teachers organization, militant and unhappy, willing to use strikes and secondary boycotts to achieve its goals, is not a prospect with much appeal. Those who think that national groups of professional educators like the American Association of School Administrators and the National Association of Secondary School Principals (both departments of the NEA) have abused their power in the past may find their record bush league stuff compared to what a truly monopolistic organization of teachers might do.

In any case, the NEA is now faced with the need to change rapidly. In 1967 its long-time executive secretary, William Carr, a pillar of the establishment, retired. There was much talk about the angry young men of the NEA and the chances for a palace revolution. Many people wondered if the younger element might be able to get one of its number into the top job. But the NEA's executive committee, which is still dominated, like the agency's other policy-making bodies, by administrators, finally opted for another establishment man, Sam Lambert, as Carr's successor. Lambert, however, will have to bend to the prevailing winds, which are no longer in favor of the old guard. And he either will have to find ways to counter and compete with the AFT, or he will have to join it. To prove that he is responsive to the demands for "teacher power" and just as militant as the next man, Lambert painted this highly colored picture of the NEA's future at his inauguration as executive secretary:

NEA last year had 1,030,000 members; and by the end of this year we will have at least 1,100,000. Within ten years our membership will exceed 2,000,000, and the great majority of these with undivided loyalties. They will be members of the profession at all levels—local and state as well as national. We are already four times as large as any other professional organization in this country. Within a few years we will be six or seven times as large. And, beginning now we are going to put our power and influence to work for the things that are most important:

NEA will become a stronger and more influential advocate of social changes long overdue

NEA will be unrelenting in seeking a better economic break for teachers in this affluent society. Our job is more important than that of a construction worker and we intend to make it pay better

NEA will become a political power second to no other special interest group. The farm bloc may have to take a back seat to the education bloc within the very near future

NEA will insist that the profession at all levels have a voice in the formulation of educational policy, in curriculum change, and in educational planning

Through its research it will continue to serve as a sounding board for teacher opinion and as a voice for the teachers on every important issue

NEA will have more and more to say about how a teacher is educated, whether he should be admitted to the profession, and depending on his behavior and ability whether he should stay in the profession. . . .

NEA will stop the old argument within its ranks over welfare versus educational leadership. Both are a necessary and vital part of our program and both will grow. . . .

And, finally, NEA will organize this profession from top to bottom into logical operating units that can move swiftly and effectively and with power unmatched by any other organized group.[3]

Tough talk that—and not particularly reassuring for all of us who would indeed like to see the NEA give more attention to teachers and less to their bosses. Many of Lambert's promises would seem to require a reduction of the influence of the administrator within the NEA and an increase of the teacher's—and so may prove illusory. Lambert may find, that is, that he cannot deliver on these promises without an unacceptable decrease in the influence of administrator groups within the organization.

Even so, the one thing that is clear in the contemporary scene is that classroom teachers, one way or another, are going to demand and get a much enhanced role in the making of school policy in America. One can only hope that they will also adopt a new militancy about the quality of education—for both students and for teachers themselves—in order to exercise their new authority with wisdom and restraint.

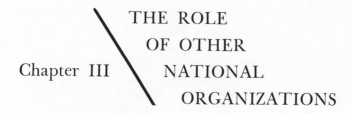

Chapter III

THE ROLE
OF OTHER
NATIONAL
ORGANIZATIONS

VISITORS FROM ABROAD are usually surprised by the coast-to-coast similarity of American schools. They have heard a lot about the decentralization and local control of our educational system and expect to see it reflected in schools. But they find that students, teachers, textbooks, schedules, curricula, and schools themselves are remarkably alike from Portland to Paducah, Atlanta to Albuquerque. Even our own educators find it easy to deceive themselves about how much freedom and diversity actually exist in American education. Freedom and diversity do indeed exist but chiefly in matters of finance and in the details of organization and administration, not in substantive questions of the curriculum or teacher training or the degree of classroom autonomy enjoyed by teachers. Other countries such as Britain that are considered far more centralized than ours exhibit more practical freedom in many important educational matters than we do. Even in France, that land of legendary rigidity in education, schools are about as free in things that really matter as are American schools.

The influence of national nongovernmental organizations in the United States accounts for much of our homogeneity. A directory published by the Office of Education lists over six hundred national and regional organizations in education and at least as many state organizations. But real power is found in relatively few of them. As we saw in the last chapter, teachers organizations are one of the main centers of nongovernmental influence in education. But other national groups, such as testing organizations, accrediting associations, and foundations also wield a good deal of control over education. Similar groups are sometimes found in other countries too but are much less important, being overshadowed by the authority of the central government. Although the power of our own federal government is greater now than ever, it is still much less in education than is true of other countries—and the role of nongovernmental national organizations correspondingly greater.

Testing Agencies

One of the many ways in which our educational system differs from that of other countries is in its lack of a national "school-leaving certificate" based on examinations. National examinations at the end of the academic secondary school are required throughout Europe by the central governments. These are public, competitive, essay exams that govern not only admission to institutions of higher education but entry to the desirable jobs in government and industry. In almost all countries, possession of the exam-based leaving certificate from the academic secondary school (the French *lycée,* the Italian *liceo,* the German or Swiss or Dutch or Swedish *gymnasium*) gives the student more or less automatic entry to any of the universities. Thus it is the central government in most other industrialized countries that decides who will go to college, not the institutions themselves. Only in Britain do the institutions control their own admissions, and even there the external pressures are such that a great deal of uniformity prevails, based on the advanced level exams of the General Certificate of Education.

Because of their importance for jobs and higher education, national exams in other countries are a major influence on educational policy. They probably have more effect on the curriculum of the secondary school than any other force. American educationists visiting Europe usually recoil at the national exam systems they see and are scandalized by what they regard as the heartless imposition of an inflexible national standard. They return home more determined than ever to preserve the pluralism and voluntarism of the American system. However, they tend to overlook the standardizing influence of our own "voluntary" testing organizations, which in their effects on schools are not so very different from the examining bodies of other countries. We may not have a government-imposed system of national exams, but we surely could be said to have a private system of national exams. It may not entirely govern admission to college but it has a very great influence on which students are admitted to most institutions. As one private school headmaster recently commented:

> Doubtless when Admiral Rickover and other irate amateurs proposed "national standard" examinations along European lines, American educators felt a perfectly genuine (and justified) thrill of horror. Yet they have increasingly and willingly ceded regulation of their guidance procedures and college applications to standardized testing programs run by two or three national, though private, organizations.[1]

Let us not try to argue here the strengths and weaknesses of the examinations which typify our national testing agencies. These exams are almost all of the multiple-choice, machine-scored variety, and for some years have been the subject of considerable debate as to whether they are reliable or whether they really test the right things. I have serious doubts about their efficacy, but our immediate concern is simply to recognize the kind of control exercised by the national testing organizations over our educational system.

The most important such organization by far is the Educational Testing Service in Princeton, New Jersey. ETS is a non-profit agency whose income of about $20,000,000 a year comes mostly from the sale of its tests. It administers the various exams of the College Entrance Examination Board (the "College Boards") and of other groups. The College Boards are, of course, the most widely used of several systems of college-entrance exams. In 1967 the College Boards were required by about seven hundred colleges and universities, which is half of our accredited, degree-granting institutions. These institutions range in quality from the best of the Ivy League to little known and pretty dubious establishments. Well over a million students, which is well over half of the entering class, take the College Boards each year.

Considering the fact that we admit over 30 percent of the age group to college, four or five times the percentage in European countries, one could say that fully as many American students, in absolute numbers or as a percentage of secondary school graduates, as European must submit to what in effect is a national exam system. But there are important differences. With us a student's College Board scores do not generally determine whether he will get a higher education, but they may determine whether or not he will go to "the college of his choice." And they have no bearing on his career if he does not go to college. In other countries a student's scores on national exams determine whether he will go to college at all, and very often whether he will get a good job if he does not go to college.

Also the "backwash" effect on the schools is different. In Europe the national exam systems are tied to published syllabuses and government study guides that sharply curtail the freedom of schools to go their own way in curricular matters. The academic secondary schools of Europe have little choice but to use the established syllabuses as the core of study for their students, though there is often considerable choice within the syllabuses and within the exams themselves. American schools have no published syllabuses to worry about and thereby enjoy, I suppose one could say, a greater measure of freedom. But this freedom may be somewhat deceptive.

Most American schools do not have a choice as to whether they will provide their best students with courses in most or all of the subjects, currently about a dozen, covered by the achievement exams of the College Boards; they must do so. Many must also provide courses adequate for other testing programs, especially for the National Merit Scholarship exams, for Advanced Placement tests, and for the tests of the American College Testing Program. These exam systems do not stipulate the content of the courses to nearly the degree that is done in Europe, but they still put definite limits around what teachers can spend their time doing and around what goes into courses that make up the college-preparatory track of our schools. Certainly schools themselves are conscious of these outside pressures and complain of them with great frequency.

Whether these pressures are good or bad is another question. It depends on whether one thinks the tests have what the professional testers call "validity" and "reliability." But it also depends on whether one feels that schools, no matter what the quality of tests, should be restrained by external forces or should have *carte blanche* to teach what they want, when and how they want it. The matter is arguable and has often been argued. My own view is that we cannot afford to let schools go their own way in the curriculum until teachers and certainly administrators are a lot better than they now are. We have in fact allowed them to do just this for a great many years with students who are *not* headed for college, who after all still make up the majority. Schools have done as they pleased with these students in the past and the results, in my view, have been bad.

I therefore see nothing but disaster in removing the pressures exerted on schools by national testing organizations. But I am by no means devoted to the multiple-choice, machine-scored type of exam that now prevails. Having looked in some detail at the European systems, I feel that we should at least experiment with an exam system that is based on the essay, and on practical demonstrations by students in such subjects as laboratory sciences and foreign languages. In short, my own conviction is that schools need the pressures of national or at least "external" exams and that such exams should apply to far more students than just the college bound; but that the tests might well be different from those now used.

Any fundamental change in the present system would require a reconstruction of college admission practices and would require the cooperation of organizations with a large financial and professional stake in the existing way of doing things. Therefore such a change is probably not feasible. The present system in all probability will be retained for the indefinite future and will, if anything, continue to expand. And standardization will continue to grow with it. In 1965 the College Boards established a "Council on College-Level Examinations," which is now developing a national system of exams for use in the placement and evaluation of students who do independent work for college, or who seek advanced standing or transfer credit, or who for whatever reason do not take other kinds of college entrance exams. Up to now, colleges have had to make their own assessments of such people and have gone about it in many different ways; now they can give up one more vestige of diversity and "go national." So whatever the flow of argument about our national testing agencies, they are probably going to remain one of the strongest influences on schools, on textbook publishing, on teaching methods, on the curriculum, and of course on higher education.

Accrediting Associations

Still another consequence of the relatively restricted authority of the federal government in education is the role assumed by national nongovernmental agencies that examine and approve—that is "accredit"—both institutions and courses of study. This function is also filled to a very limited extent by state governments, but it is the national and regional accrediting organizations that have the real power. In other countries the national government maintains, usually in the ministry of education, a corps of inspectors who act as accreditors by visiting and reporting on schools and other educational establishments. The inspectorate is the eyes and ears of the central government; it is an important means of maintaining national standards; it is a means of promoting new ideas and spreading the word about successful experiments; it is a guardian of tax moneys; it is an evaluator of teachers, administrators, and schools. No other country has the sort of accreditation bodies that prevail in the United States for the approval of schools and colleges.

In higher education the central government in other countries relies on informal methods of inspection and appraisal (except for teachers colleges, which are usually covered by the ministry's inspectorate). Universities are much less numerous and various in Europe than in the United States, with far fewer programs of study and with a much more homogeneous student body whose members have all qualified for admission by virtue of possessing the national leaving certificate from the academic secondary school. Universities abroad are therefore not subject to anything like the external influences that accrediting bodies exercise over American institutions of higher education.

Accreditation, then, is a process by which nongovernmental professional organizations define the standards and criteria that institutions wanting their stamp of approval must meet. The criteria apply sometimes to the whole institution but more often to a particular program or degree. Institutions are generally given full or provisional approval by accrediting bodies but are not "rated" on any sort of scale or in any public or comparative way. They are subject to various kinds of punitive action if they fall below minimum standards after being accredited. The most severe penalty is disaccreditation, an action that has grave consequences for institutions and their students and is rarely invoked.

Currently there are over two dozen accrediting agencies that our colleges and universities must deal with, covering everything from veterinary medicine to Bible study. An institution's programs and degrees in law, theology, forestry, dentistry, podiatry, medicine, architecture, psychology, librarianship, music, optometry, social work, teacher training, and other fields are subject to accreditation by outside, nongovernmental agencies. Each field is covered by a separate accrediting organization, and each organization demands extensive reporting from the institution. Each sends official visitors, often a team of them, to the

campus to examine the quality of work done, and each supposedly keeps an eye on its accredited institutions between official
visits.

Accrediting groups multiplied after World War II at such a
rate that college administrators, finding too much of their time
and the institution's money being consumed by such groups,
began to make loud noises about restricting this proliferation.
The result was the formation in 1950 of the National Commission on Accrediting, an agency that in effect accredits accrediting
agencies. It attempts both to improve the quality of accrediting
bodies and to keep their number within reasonable limits.

In addition to specialized, professional agencies of the sort
mentioned above, there are regional organizations that cover
both secondary schools and colleges and that accredit the entire
institution rather than particular programs. It is their stamp of
approval that most people have in mind when they speak of
an institution's being "fully accredited." Six regional agencies
blanket the United States and its territories; they accredit many
thousands of secondary schools and over 1,600 institutions of
higher education. The six range in size from the Northwest Association of Secondary and Higher Schools, with fewer than one
hundred institutions of higher education on its accredited list,
to the North Central Association of Colleges and Secondary
Schools with over five hundred. The latter, covering nineteen
mid-continent states, also has nearly 4,000 secondary schools on
its accredited list.

Most laymen are probably unaware that public high schools
and a great many private secondary schools are subject to the
extralegal accreditation of regional associations as well as to
state approval. The accreditation process, however, varies a good
deal among the six regional associations. Some accredit high
schools on the basis of institutional reports and regular, albeit
widely spaced, visits; some on the basis of reports only; some on
the basis of an initial visit only. At the largest of the regionals,
the North Central Association, accreditation for high schools takes
place mostly on paper; the schools, that is, submit written re-

ports each year to North Central and on the basis of these reports are continued on the accredited list.

North Central's standards are highly quantified and somewhat mechanical, and, in my view, of dubious validity. Only high schools that get into trouble or are borderline institutions are actually visited by North Central. On these occasions the accrediting organization can make life very difficult for the schools, especially when it rigidly insists on standards that in themselves are controversial or without a demonstrable relation to educational quality. North Central has managed to arouse the fighting resentment of parents on a number of occasions in the past because of its authoritarian behavior.

The majority of public high schools in all regions of the country are members of their regional associations. So are the majority of private schools (except Roman Catholic institutions) in the New England and Mid-Atlantic regions. While there is no compulsion for a school to belong to its regional association, most schools feel the same sort of pressure to join as do the colleges and universities. They really don't have a choice, even though they may not approve of the way the regionals go about their business. Without attempting here to go into the details of high school accreditation, I would point out that accredited status for any given school says no more about its quality than it does with colleges. It is possible that high school accreditation is now carried out in so questionable a manner that the public would be better served if its schools did not have to seek any sort of regional approval.

 How much influence do accrediting bodies have on education? A very great deal. Collectively and often individually they can dictate educational policy. In higher education the accredited label of the regional associations is coveted by our institutions and in fact is indispensable to most of them; it is the minimum criterion, wisely or not, used by parents in choosing a college, by employers in hiring the school's graduates, by government departments and by foundations in dispensing grants and contracts, and by the general public in assessing the institution.

The accredited label in many of the professional fields is even more important.

In other words the faith that *other* people have in accreditation, and the uses to which people outside the institutions put it, gives the accrediting agencies their power. These agencies can therefore bring irresistible pressure to bear on institutions to force them to conform to what people outside the institutions think are desirable practices in matters of faculty, budget, instruction, facilities, or most other matters of moment in education.

How wisely this power has been wielded is another matter. One could put together a large volume of case histories to demonstrate the abuse of power by accrediting bodies, of instances of discrimination and arbitrary rulings, of rigid procedures and obtuse officials. More important is the question of whether accreditation is a good or bad thing for our colleges in general. My own opinion is that accreditation in some fields in higher education has been an important means of maintaining quality, but that in the areas that cover the greatest number of institutions and students it has done more harm than good and ought now to be ended or radically transformed.

Let me take two examples to illustrate briefly the failings I have in mind: the regional associations, which accredit entire institutions; and the National Council for Accreditation of Teacher Education, which accredits programs in professional education, the largest single segment of our system of higher education. My quarrel with the regionals is twofold. First, their stamp of approval is meaningless because it does not discriminate between the best and the worst, and therefore misleads all those people who think it does. The accredited list of any of the regional associations includes many institutions that by any reasonable standard of quality are less than mediocre. For them to enjoy the same stamp of approval as our best institutions means that approval is easily won and therefore suspect.

Of course the accredited lists also include the names of our strongest institutions, but they are not strong because they are accredited; accreditation for them is simply irrelevant. But for the weaker institutions it is a vehicle of misinformation. The regionals almost never disaccredit an institution once it is on the approved list, no matter how far it may have drifted downhill between visits, which are often a decade or more apart. Nor have the regionals ever saved the country from out-and-out diploma mills, of which we have more than any other nation. It is surely a sad irony that, for example, the largest of our regional accrediting associations is headquartered in Chicago, a city notable for its diploma mills, and is helpless to do anything about them.

Second, the "standards and criteria" created by the regionals and imposed on the institutions that seek accreditation are too often vague and arguable and not demonstrably related to academic quality. A look, for instance, at the North Central's "Guide for the Evaluation of Institutions of Higher Education" would impress any layman, I believe, by the lack of specificity of many items that are supposed to be judged by visiting teams, and by the imprecision inherent in any attempt to evaluate something like "the intellectual climate of the institution." Moreover, where the guide *is* specific, as it is in endless details of administration, one finds it hard to see the validity of the requirements or their necessary connection with academic quality. The following statement, typical enough of those that come from accrediting agencies, is italicized in a pamphlet of the National Commission on Accrediting that is aimed at foreign visitors, who have no way of evaluating the claim:

> . . . *while the graduation requirements of accredited colleges and universities in the United States are not identical, it can be assumed that the degrees awarded by all accredited institutions meet at least a common minimum level of quality.*[2]

If that is true, the "common minimum level of quality" is so low as to make regional accreditation useless as a guide to quality. That indeed is my belief.

These problems of accreditation are seen even more clearly with the National Council for Accreditation of Teacher Education (NCATE), one of the largest and most powerful of the professional agencies that accredit particular subjects or degrees. "Teacher education" in our colleges and universities is a gigantic industry involving a great variety of degrees and training programs for teachers, school administrators, future professors of education, and sundry other persons and specialists in education. Most people are wholly unaware of the fact, for example, that nearly four out of every ten persons who take the bachelor's degree each year from our institutions of higher education have been through the teacher-training program of their institutions. Nearly half of all the master's degrees awarded each year in the United States are awarded in the field of education. And more doctorate degrees are awarded each year in education than in any other field.

NCATE is the only national agency that accredits this multitude of training programs—programs that are among the biggest money makers on many an American campus and whose administrators therefore have a major voice in academic policy. Between 75 and 80 percent of all new teachers these days are prepared in NCATE-accredited institutions. NCATE thus enjoys a degree of leverage over educational programs and policy that probably cannot be matched by any other single agency in the country.

But like the regionals, NCATE may well do more harm than good. It became a highly controversial agency in the early 1960's, partly because of its monopolistic power and the narrowness of its policies, but mostly because it was an organization of, by, and for the professional establishment. Most of its financing came from the NEA—from the so-called TEPS Commission (National Commission on Teacher Education and Professional Standards), an NEA organization, and the American Association of Colleges for Teacher Education, a department of the NEA. The board that controlled NCATE was almost exclusively made up of professional educators and establishment figures. The "Standards and Criteria" developed by NCATE and imposed without flexibility or imagination on applying institutions were irksome to the liberal arts departments, which considered them anti-intellectual and "teachers college trivia."

But most of all, NCATE was criticized for its power politics. It was censured for pressuring institutions into applying for accreditation, for encouraging professional associations of various kinds to restrict their membership to graduates of NCATE-accredited programs, for persuading their fellow professional educators in state departments of education to discriminate against teachers who applied for a license from non-NCATE schools—in a word, for seeking to build a giant, coercive monopoly governed by professional educators in a field that involved the entire college or university.

In response to this criticism, which came particularly from scholarly associations, from the Council for Basic Education, from liberal arts colleges, and from individuals like James Bryant Conant, NCATE undertook some internal reforms in the mid-1960's that are still in the process of implementation. Some effort was made to create standards that would be more acceptable to liberal arts departments, and some steps taken to bring at least a semblance of the democratic process into the making of NCATE policy. These reforms will probably modify the unsavory reputation that NCATE was rapidly building among the better colleges and among academic people generally, but it remains to be seen whether the reforms will actually be carried out and will have any real teeth in them.

NCATE still gets over half of its budget from the two NEA groups mentioned above; its main policy-making board is still dominated by professional educators just as it was in the past. Its standards of accreditation are still narrow and inelastic and, more important, not related in any measurable way to the quality of people turned out of the training programs. And other groups, such as the powerful American Association of School Administrators, still use NCATE as a bludgeon with which to beat all preparing institutions into line, simply by refusing membership to anybody not a graduate of an NCATE school. Also, informal and off-the-record pressures of many kinds are still brought to bear on behalf of NCATE by people in strategic positions, such as state officials who issue licenses to teachers, or local administrators who hire them. In short NCATE still dominates the largest part of our system of higher education and is worth the close attention of anybody who thinks the old establishment is losing its grip.

But we cannot hope to settle here, or even to throw much light on, the complex issues surrounding the world of accreditation in American education. I have tried only to indicate what some of the issues are. Our main concern is to note the kinds of control exercised by these agencies over the educational system. In all probability their power will become even stronger in the future.

Curriculum Reform Groups

In 1967 the United States could look back on a mere fifteen years—in most respects only a decade—of one of the most remarkable movements in our educational history: the movement in which the academic scholar became reinvolved in public school affairs and in which a large number of them have collaborated with teachers from the schools to effect fundamental reform of the school curriculum. Before this movement began, control of the curriculum of American schools, the subjects taught and their content, was atomized among many people and groups. Control was occasionally in the hands of teachers, but more often of educational administrators and nonteaching "curriculum specialists"; in any case it was certainly not in the hands of university academicians.

Before the present movement the most frequent complaint of people who criticized the schools was the lack of content in the curriculum, a condition they often ascribed to the absence of scholars from public school affairs and to the empire building of professional educators. A beginning of reform was made in 1952 when a small group of professional mathematicians from the

universities and of teachers from the schools was established under the leadership of Max Beberman at the University of Illinois. Their object was to overhaul the teaching of mathematics
in the schools and to see if students could be made to emerge
from the schools with an understanding of and an enthusiasm
for mathematics, something that was not then true of most
students.

A few years later a larger project was established in another
school subject at MIT with the formation of its well known
Physical Science Study Committee (PSSC), which aimed at a
complete reconstruction of the high school physics course. PSSC
was followed in the 1960's by still other projects and other reform groups, in chemistry, biology, foreign languages, and social
studies.

In chemistry there is the Chemical Education Material Study
which has created a radically new high school course through the
joint efforts of the American Chemical Society, the University of
California, and Harvey Mudd College. There is the Chemical
Bond Approach Project, which has developed high school materials around the theme of chemical bonding. In biology there
is the Biological Sciences Curriculum Study, which has produced
no fewer than three separate and distinct courses in high school
biology, all of them sharply different from the traditional school
course. In science for the elementary school, at least three important groups of scholars and teachers are at work: the Science Curriculum Improvement Study, the Elementary School Science
Project, and the Elementary Science Study. For the junior high
school, there is the Introductory Physical Science group, among
others. In mathematics, of course, many curriculum reform groups
have been working for a number of years. In particular the Educational Research Council of Greater Cleveland has turned out
the "new math" that is most widely used in the elementary school,
and the School Mathematics Study Group at Stanford University,
which has produced over a hundred volumes of materials, is the
most widely used in the high school.

Still other groups are now extending curriculum reform into

areas not generally considered academic, such as vocational education. By 1967 most of the basic academic subjects were undergoing fundamental reform in content and method by groups made up of teachers from the schools and outstanding faculty members from the liberal arts departments of our colleges and universities. Even subjects that for years remained stubbornly untouched by the curriculum reform movement, such as English (perhaps the most important of all school subjects) and geography are now in at least the beginning stages of reform. The consequences for American education of this kind of unparalleled curriculum reform have already been great and will be much greater in the near future as the new courses are adopted widely and teachers trained to use the new materials.

Although I cannot hope to discuss these many reform groups here, I can perhaps indicate their significance and their mode of operation by looking in more detail at PSSC, the group that was the inspiration for many of the succeeding curriculum projects.

PSSC began with a memo on March 15, 1956, from a distinguished MIT physicist, Jerrold Zacharias, to James R. Killian, then president of MIT. In it Zacharias proposed an experiment to see if the teaching of high school physics could be improved through the production by outstanding scientists of ninety short films with accompanying textbooks and other materials. Why did he and many of his fellow physicists feel that the subject needed improvement? For the same reason that college teachers of other subjects had felt for a long time that their subjects also needed improvement in the high schools: the poor preparation of students who appeared fresh from the schools year after year in their classes.

Other reasons were also important to people who later became involved in PSSC. There was, for example, a great deal of talk in the country about the superiority of Russian science. There was also concern about the public's ignorance of science and about the tendency of people to blame scientists for threatening the world with incineration. There was also the desire to convey to high school students the sheer delight that scientists felt in science. Most of all there was the fact that many academic people shared Zacharias' conviction that, as he put it, "our real problem as a nation was creeping anti-intellectualism, from which came many of our educational deficiencies."

Zacharias's memo brought an initial grant from the National Science Foundation which enabled some of the world's best known physicists to be brought together at the end of 1956 to review the materials most often used then in high school physics (they failed to find any satisfactory textbooks or films) and to hammer out plans for a new course. PSSC was created, and over the next few years NSF and private foundations kept it running to the tune of $1,400,000 a year. The size is important because it was a new way to tackle an old problem. Zacharias's work during World War II at MIT's Radiation Lab and on the Manhattan Project demonstrated to him the kind of scientific progress that could be made in a short time when a well financed and sufficiently massive attack is made on a problem by first-rate people, and he saw no reason why the same results could not be obtained in education.

Thus PSSC represented the first attempt in the history of American education to bring classroom teachers together on a large scale with eminent academicians, including Nobel laureates, and to give them enough money to allow them a lengthy period of time for the creation, the trying out in schools, and then for the re-creation of a complete new course of study in the high school: a course that is a complete curriculum package made up of a textbook, many films, monographs, tests, and inexpensive apparatus. For many years before PSSC came into being, other voices had been crying in the wilderness about the need to reform the public school curriculum and to give the best scholars from the universities, who knew the most about the subjects involved, a major voice in curriculum development; but few people did more than talk about it and fewer still thought about it on the required scale.

Today high school physics is wholly different from what it was before PSSC. At least a quarter of the students who study physics in our public schools study PSSC physics. Moreover, PSSC gave rise to other reform groups in the same subject that are now developing contrasting and competing courses in high school physics to be studied by students not taking PSSC.

PSSC proved to be only the beginning for Zacharias and his Boston-based group of reformers. In 1958 they created an organization called Educational Services Incorporated, which served as the administrative umbrella under which PSSC could operate, as well as other projects that followed in PSSC's image, for it was soon clear to the PSSC group that curriculum reform was needed as badly in other subjects as in physics.

ESI set up shop in a converted supermarket in a Boston suburb and soon began to collect other curriculum projects. PSSC led to a concern for elementary school science, and in 1960 a project in this critical area was launched at ESI. These two projects soon led to one in college physics, and that to one in engineering education. Soon there was an extensive African Education Program—a project that grew out of the dismay Zacharias felt upon attending a conference in Israel on science in underdeveloped countries and finding most of the delegates talking about nuclear reactors and giant hydroelectric plants instead of about the inescapable prerequisite of a developed educational system.

In 1962 ESI expanded its activities beyond the sciences and put together a large curriculum project in that no man's land of American education, the social sciences. Still other projects at all educational levels came rapidly along until today there are no fewer than thirty projects running, including a dozen in ESI's remarkable film studio, the best of its kind in the country. ESI has a staff of four hundred persons, and its yearly budget approaches $11,000,000. Thus ESI is by far the largest organization in the country devoting itself to research and development in curriculum, and is still quite unique in the kinds and combinations of people, representing a variety of occupations and professions by no means restricted to education, who work with it.

Looking at all this growth, some of which was deliberately sought by ESI and some of which came in the form of outside requests, one might easily see it as a classic example of the familiar phenomenon of educational empire building. Perhaps it is, but of education's many empires this is surely one of the most important.

ESI, however, no longer exists under that name. In January 1967 it merged, as I mentioned in Chapter I, with another organization to become Education Development Center, an agency that carries on all of the ESI projects mentioned above and that also operates the regional educational laboratory in New England. Because I became associated with EDC at the end of 1967, the reader may want to take my evaluation of ESI-EDC with caution. I feel that the organization is the largest, best equipped, most experienced, and most promising agency in curriculum development in the country. Although it may have spent a lot of money badly, it has also spent a lot well. I don't know that any other educational agency would have spent it better or as well. I don't feel that all of the courses it has developed should be adopted by all or even most schools, but I feel that it has developed some excellent materials not matched by any other group. Most of all, I feel that its historical role and its accumulated experience doing pioneer work in American education are of great significance. Without EDC—which is to say without its predecessor groups, PSSC and ESI—there probably would have been no regional educational laboratories (possibly no great loss), and probably a curriculum reform movement of much less scope than the present one (which would have been a great loss indeed).

Because of that movement the greatest part of the school curriculum will ultimately be overhauled and modernized. The movement has already had a marked effect on educational policy and practice, at least if one is to judge by such signs as the quantity of textbooks published and purchased in the "new curricula," by the records of high school students now entering college, by questionnaires returned from teachers and administrators, and by the amount of public and professional attention given the reform groups. It seems evident that most students in most schools will soon be studying the new courses for some portion of their time and for a substantial part in the years immediately ahead. So in the space of ten years a complete transformation has taken place in some of the most important school subjects, and a similar change is well under way in half a dozen other academic subjects. In a nation without a ministry of education or centralized educational authority, that is an unprecedented achievement.

In his second look at the high schools, James Bryant Conant surveyed a number of medium-sized comprehensive schools by questionnaire and reported as follows:

> We asked whether the school in question was offering one or more of the new courses in chemistry, physics, and biology (all the schools were offering instruction in these subjects). It turned out that about half of all the schools responding have adopted the new physics, about half the new chemistry, and over half (64.9 percent) one of the new biology courses.[3]

If anyone had suggested a decade ago that any significant percentage of American students would now be studying radically new academic courses, put together by established scholars and school teachers, he would hardly have been taken seriously. The number of such students may soon be approaching half in the high schools, and large but undetermined numbers in the elementary schools. Whether by design or not, the curriculum reform movement has effected a certain shift in the politics of our educational system: it has restored the academician, who used to be thought of by professional educators as dreamy and ill-informed about schools, to a central role in curriculum development, one of the most important roles in education.

Foundations

The private philanthropic foundation, nonprofit and tax exempt, flourishes in the United States as in no other country, and education is its biggest activity. Thanks to our tax laws, the number of foundations increases steadily. In 1966 we had 6,803 that met one or both of the following criteria: They made grants of at least $10,000 a year or, they had assets of at least $200,000. Collectively these foundations, which require a 1,200-page reference volume just for the recording of basic facts about them, have nearly 20 billion dollars in assets and give away well over a billion dollars a year.[4] In addition there are thousands of small foundations, often family controlled, that spend much of their money on education.

In trying to assess the influence that our foundations have on education, we have to settle for a less specific judgment than most of us would like. My own conviction is that foundations do indeed exercise a major influence and that without them American education would be different from what it is. Almost every area of education has been fundamentally affected within the last fifteen years by foundation-sponsored work. Projects in curriculum reform, in teacher training, testing, school finance, buildings, educational television, teaching machines, team teaching, public information and citizens groups, all have received substantial support from our foundations for the purpose of developing new ideas—for trying to effect, that is, some reforms in education. The Ford Foundation alone has spent over $65,000,000 since 1951 on new kinds of programs for the training of school teachers, mostly Master of Arts in Teaching programs, and has made thereby a permanent difference in one of the most change-resistant areas of our educational system. The Carnegie Corporation in recent years has created with relatively modest grants such bodies as the Compact for Education, the Committee on Assessing the Progress of Education, and the Commission of Educational Television, all of which promise to have a substantial influence on education.

Suppose we look in more detail at a current example of an unorthodox foundation-supported project that demonstrates the role played by major foundations, the Carnegie assessment project. The impetus to this project, known as the "National Assessment of Educational Progress," came from Francis Keppel during his administration of the United States Office of Education. In 1963 he pointed out to John W. Gardner, then president of the Carnegie Corporation, that the Commissioner of Education had been required since 1867 by the Congress to report regularly to the nation on the progress of education, but that no instruments had ever been created to allow him to make such an assessment.

The United States, as I mentioned earlier, is the only advanced country of the world without a national system of public examinations and, except for the State of New York, without a school-leaving certificate based on examinations. Thus we have found ourselves, as a nation that spends far more money, absolutely and per capita, than any other on education, in the awkward and frustrating position of not knowing much about the results achieved with our enormous expenditures. Such ignorance has many ill effects, not least in preventing the commissioner of education or anybody else from making a comprehensive annual evaluation of the schools.

Carnegie responded to Keppel's complaint by sponsoring a series of conferences at which questions about the feasibility and desirability of some kind of national testing or assessment were discussed and answered affirmatively. Carnegie then appointed a high-level committee to develop the means and methods by which a national assessment could be carried out. Working slowly and with great caution, this committee over the last few years has supervised a laborious process by which the objectives of American schools were identified (and ratified by laymen), trial tests prepared by established test-making agencies, and large-scale trials carried out in schools. As I write, the project is nearing the end of the test-trial phase, and preliminary reports from it are encouraging. They presumably will lead to the first phase of the main national assessment in the 1968–69 academic year. By the end of 1971, the entire project should be completed and should produce a far greater fund of knowledge than anything we have ever had before, not only about American educational standards, but about the technical aspects of mass testing.

With a fear that is all too well grounded, the committee has avoided like poison any talk about "national testing" or any suggestion about producing data with which individual students or schools or even states could be ranked or compared. The committee has produced a plan whereby the country will be divided into four regions and the only geographical comparisons possible will be regional. Within these four regions, a battery of tests will be given to a probability sample of four age groups: 9, 13, 17, and adults under 30. Further classifications will be made by sex, socio-economic status, and type of community.

The tests to be given will include "language arts," reading, science, mathematics, social studies, citizenship, fine arts, and vocational education. In addition there will be demonstration tests and interviews. The sample is so constructed that no individual will take all or even most of the "exercises," as the committee in its politic reticence calls the tests. Hence results will yield information of the following sort:

> Among 17-year-old girls of higher socio-economic status from rural and small town areas in the Midwest region, it was found that – percent could read a typical newspaper paragraph similar to the following example . . . and that – percent could write an acceptable letter similar to the following example. . . .

The committee's caution would seem excessive, even laughable, to a British or European educator long accustomed to the comparative uses to which national tests are put, and often beneficially put. But many people in American education, especially school administrators, react viscerally to the slightest suggestion of any kind of national testing or national curriculum, and in particular to any proposal that might make it possible for comparisons between schools to be made. They say they fear unfair comparisons by uninformed or malicious people, but one can't escape the feeling that it may be competition they really fear.

Administrators tend to see these threats the way other people see Communists: under every academic bed. Witness the manner in which the American Association of School Administrators responded to the assessment project. At the AASA's 1966 annual convention, one of the big affairs in education, various association leaders excoriated the project in astonishing ignorance of what the project proposed to do. In advance of its 1967 convention, the AASA's executive committee, having failed to do its homework for an entire year, got out another ill-informed broadside to its membership officially denouncing the project and recommending that AASA members refuse to let their schools be used for it.

This boycott, if it had been adopted by the AASA, would probably have killed the project. Fortunately, the shocked reaction of large segments of the public and the education community, including some individual AASA members, to this head-in-the-sand attitude caused the main 1967 convention to repudiate the executive committee's recommendation. And so this unique project in educational evaluation goes forward and has received the support of almost all laymen and scholars who have taken the trouble to understand it. The NEA hierarchy remains hostile to it but may have to modify its opposition because of the weight of public and professional opinion. When the project is completed we may at last have available some reliable information about what it is we are buying for the many billions of dollars we spend each year on public education. And national assessment may become a permanent part of the educational scene for the first time in our history.

Such a controversial project could not have been developed in our country by the Office of Education or any other government agency. Nor would it have been feasible for institutions of higher education or other kinds of nongovernmental educational organizations. It could have been sponsored and developed only by the kind of body that we fortunately have in large numbers and that other nations lack—the philanthropic foundation.

One could easily argue that our foundations on the whole have not been as imaginative or daring as they could have been. If they represent society's "risk capital," as they like to claim, one could say that most of their educational programs have not really been very risky compared to what they might have been. Nor have the larger foundations always been successful. The Kellogg Foundation, for example, has pumped many millions of dollars into projects to improve the training of school administrators, with no noticeable improvement in that art. All of us like to think we could have spent foundation funds much more productively in education than has been the case, but the fact remains that our foundations are one of the most effective means we have for the reform of education.

One should remember to look beyond the dozen largest foundations. Hundreds of substantial grants are made in education by "smaller" foundations every year, and many of them support programs that have some national significance. They also support thousands of individual students, researchers, and institutions. The total expenditures of foundations may be only a tiny fraction of what the nation spends on education, but that fraction often affects the whole. In brief, American foundations are one of the main national influences in education and will continue to be unless they are overwhelmed by the expenditures of the federal government, with whom they obviously cannot compete, although they will always enjoy more freedom of action than any government agency.

Citizens Advisory Groups

On the local scene voluntary educational associations of parents and laymen come and go in large numbers, but not many groups of national significance now exist. The two largest groups, the National School Boards Association and the National Congress of Parents and Teachers, are more important at the state and local level than nationally, and I therefore defer my discussion of them until later. Suffice it here to say that these groups find it hard to exert a national influence because of the extremely mixed nature of their membership and the consequent difficulty their officials have of arriving at an institutional point of view that is something other than bland; also because they have been too much under the influence in the past of the professional establishment and have failed to be the independent national voice they might have been.

Other national groups, though smaller and more ephemeral than the two above, frequently have a surprising influence. One of the remarkable developments, for example, after World War II, was the formation of a national citizens organization that became the impetus to the creation of innumerable community groups. It was the National Citizens Commission for the Public Schools, established with foundation support in 1949 by a number of prominent men and women. Its main purpose was to promote improvement in the schools through public discussion of educational problems, through workshops, and through printed literature. It established a number of regional offices and helped in the founding of a great many other citizens groups with the same general purpose.

The NCCPS may have been an illustration of Victor Hugo's dictum about the power of an idea whose time has come, for it became the best known citizens group in our educational history. Although it was primarily a lay organization, the NCCPS failed to tax the educational establishment with its failures and deficiencies, which were, after all, one of the chief reasons for the creation of the NCCPS in the first place. Instead it demonstrated a high degree of gullibility by devoting itself to projects that were acceptable to the professionals, and thereby became known as an unadventuresome but blue-ribbon organization that did good by bringing schools into public consciousness. It was also instrumental in creating the White House Conference on Education in 1955, a conference that was wholly controlled by the professional establishment. No doubt NCCPS did succeed in making many laymen aware of educational problems and in getting them involved in looking for answers. It disbanded in 1956 but was immediately succeeded by another organization called the National Citizens Council for Better Schools. The NCCBS carried on in much the same vein as its predecessor but slowly ran out of steam and money and ultimately dissolved.

I mention the NCCPS only to put present groups into perspective. Currently one finds only a few citizens groups of national significance in operation, none of them as notable as NCCPS. There is the National Committee for Support of the Public Schools, a Washington-based organization formed in 1962 by a group of well known persons responding to an invitation from Agnes Meyer, a philanthropist who had also been active in the NCCPS, and Harold Taylor, known for his espousal of various brands of progressive education and progressive causes. In contrast to other citizens groups, NCSPS has a single, concrete aim: to get more money for the public schools and get it distributed more equitably than is now the case.

In practice NCSPS's activities are very broad, for almost anything can be made relevant to its goal of creating "through the spread of ideas and information, a climate of opinion in which citizens will demand and work for an adequately financed public educational system." Thus NCSPS sponsors meetings and produces publications on such sensitive topics as national standards, teacher training, testing, professional organizations, the general quality of American education, as well as on school finance. It has over a thousand members (who pay no dues), including a number of well known people from a variety of backgrounds and occupations. Although NCSPS is a lay organization that has sometimes criticized the establishment, it gets along pretty well with the professionals since its main goal is to persuade Americans, through improving their understanding of education, to spend more money on schools. Its influence is not measurable, of course, but NCSPS probably has helped to condition the national temper to greater educational expenditures. These expenditures have been rising at a dramatic rate and now exceed those of any other industrialized country.

A second organization of current interest is the National Center for Citizens in Education. It owes its existence to one of the oldest and most important state citizens groups, the New York State Citizens Committee for the Public Schools. The National Center is mostly concerned with the preparation and dissemination of literature. In particular it distributes a series of "Community Counseling Kits" for the guidance of local citizens groups. It acts as a clearing house for information about the work of state and local citizens groups in education and as a library and reference service for such groups. It distributes large quantities of educational literature and probably does have some effect on the course of our schools.

Still another national lay agency is the Council for Basic Education in Washington, D.C. I cannot pretend to any sort of detached judgment about CBE, for I have been associated with it in one way or another since its inception in 1956; but perhaps I can record the main facts and some opinions. CBE is a unique organization that was born out of the pre-Sputnik concern of a number of outstanding people of diverse backgrounds about the quality of American education. Although its members differ widely on other public questions, they all have in common a belief in the importance of an education for all students that is centered in the basic subjects, in English, history, geography, foreign languages, the physical sciences, and the arts. They are drawn together not only by this goal, but also by their rejection of progressive education as it was carried out in the schools for the greater part of this century. Their chief conviction is that the promise of universal education can only be realized through systematic study by all students in the fundamental areas of human knowledge, and that other subjects and activities should be subordinated to this aim. CBE pursues its goal through publications, information services, and special studies, and through the individual activities of many of its members.

Again, one can assess the council's influence only in very general terms. I believe that CBE has made a difference in the twelve years of its existence. It has been a consistent force at the national level in helping to shape public attitudes about education; and through its monthly *Bulletin* has provided the public with one of the most literate and urbane publications in education. As the only organization of its kind in the country, it has steadily kept the need for educational reform before the public. It has been a useful and badly needed thorn in the side of orthodoxy and the professional establishment, and a source of encouragement to teachers and administrators who have opposed the status quo and worked for change. And change there has been in our educational system in the last decade.

Other national citizens groups are sometimes influential in special ways. The Reading Reform Foundation, for instance, has probably had some influence on a specific educational problem: how to break the monopolistic grip that the look-and-say method of teaching reading has had on American schools and to reestablish phonics instruction at least as an alternative method. But in general we are not rich in effective lay groups at the national level. Neither are other countries, most of which have even fewer than we do. We need more but are unlikely to get them.

Other National Groups and Influences

We cannot say much about the effect that other national bodies, most of them not primarily concerned with education, have on educational policy. But we can at least acknowledge their existence and perhaps say a word about their possible influence. Consider the publishing industry, for example a large and growing business. No matter how much we may talk about the present and the future impact of educational technology, or how much validity we think there may be in McLuhanism, the fact remains that textbooks and other printed teaching materials remain the principal instrument with which education is conducted.

The influence of textbooks and publishers on educational policy and standards may be subterranean, but it pervades the school system. The teaching of reading, to return for a moment to that tormented subject, has been strongly conditioned by the nearly exclusive promotion of look-and-say readers by the major publishers. A cynic might say that there has been a kind of closed shop in reading, a collusion between publishers and reading experts to exploit and protect a big textbook market. Some of our major institutions such as Teachers College (Columbia University) must also bear a good deal of responsibility for this monopoly, as must California and other states where statewide textbook adoptions in reading have often been limited to look-and-say materials.

Only in the last few years have a few publishers moved into phonics readers and begun to push them. Many publishers still have enormous investments in look-and-say, as do numerous reading experts, most of them professors of education with substantial royalties from look-and-say reading systems. The effect of these vested interests has been to perpetuate a system of reading instruction that many people feel is demonstrably inferior. One could no doubt hold, and I would, that the real failure is not that of the publishing industry or of avaricious experts, but of teachers and schools, and teachers of teachers, who have not demanded something better, who have been either indifferent to the problem or who have been bamboozled by the garish rhetoric of the experts.[5] Publishers, after all, are quite willing and anxious to meet any demand that is sufficiently profitable. But the failure of teachers to demand or to create better materials has made the publishers a major influence in promoting a single method for the teaching of the most important of all school subjects.

Publishers have been equally influential, and for the same reason, in such areas as history where their products have frequently been bland and chauvinistic (and dull), in science and mathematics where they have been obsolete, in "social studies" where they have been puerile. Fortunately the publishing industry, in response to the curriculum reform movement, is now doing better, and its influence may become a force for good. But good or bad, its impact on education should not be underestimated.

Closely allied with publishing is the new field of educational technology. The manufacturing and marketing of teaching machines, of computers for classroom use, of language laboratories, of films and tapes, and sundry other products based on applications of electronics to education, constitute another growth industry that seeks in one way or another to influence educational policy. A great many corporations and commercial organizations —IBM, Time, General Electric, Westinghouse, Burroughs, Litton Industries, Bell and Howell, Philco-Ford, Minnesota Mining, General Dynamics, American Telephone and Telegraph, Raytheon, RCA, CBS, Goodyear, Reader's Digest, Encyclopaedia Britannica, Walt Disney Productions—these and many others have moved smartly into the "knowledge industry" in the last few years. They often do so by merging with publishing houses with the aim of developing innovative products for what they believe will soon be a market second in size only to national defense.

The impact to date of this new technology has not been great in the schools. Part of the trouble has been the hasty claims and the hucksterish promotion by the industry—"artificial dissemination," as some people call it—and quick disillusionment in the schools. Teachers and administrators, moreover, have often felt unable to evaluate the new products of educational technology, or have been intimidated and overwhelmed by them. Whereas James Bryant Conant, in his 1966 review of progress in the high schools, found a majority of them using one or more of the new courses that have come out of the curriculum reform groups, he found only a small minority using either educational television or programmed instruction.

But clearly the potential application of technology to education is tremendous. How long it will take for the era of high-pressure selling of "hardware" and unsophisticated buying to pass remains to be seen. Educators would do well to stop talking about the incompatibility of education and the profit motive and, guarded by the maxim, *caveat emptor,* develop the means for evaluating the products of educational technology. If they do not, they will have to be prepared to see industry itself exerting an ever greater influence on school policy.

National religious groups, of course, are also to be reckoned with. Both Roman Catholic and Protestant organizations, though not registered lobbyists, can often affect congressional decisions in education by their position on pending legislation. One of the main forces behind the defeat of the 1961 proposal for federal aid to education was the National Council of Churches, which opposed the giving of tax moneys to parochial schools. The influence of national church organizations is still one of the chief obstacles to general, unrestricted federal aid to education, just as the opposition of Roman Catholic groups to general aid to *public* schools remains a big congressional obstacle. Whether a compromise can be reached in the future is a moot point. One of the main reasons the voters of New York State voted down the whole of a new state constitution in November 1967 was the fact that Protestant groups felt it contained a loose provision permitting tax funds to go to Roman Catholic and other private schools. A similar fate may be in store for congressional bills that propose unrestricted federal aid to private schools.

Nor should we overlook other national influences, such as the press itself. Coverage of education in the mass media has increased sharply since Sputnik, and educational journalism is becoming a recognized specialty. In contrast to the situation ten years ago, most of the major daily newspapers now have at least one full-time education reporter, and few, if any, are without a reporter who gives a substantial part of his time to education.

The national press does not speak with a single voice, of course, and seldom has an effect on educational policy that can be measured. But I would guess that its effect on education is considerable in conditioning public discussion, and is mostly on the side of reform. Its attention, that is, naturally gravitates to what is newsworthy in education, and that results in articles that criticize the status quo or in statements from people who are making demands for change.

Educational reporting is still a long way from what it could be: a reliable guide for laymen to what is happening in education and a steady source of informed analysis. Sometimes the national press unjustly pillories a movement or an institution and sometimes whitewashes it. Sometimes the local press refuses to print material critical of the schools; sometimes it goes to the other extreme and carries on a vendetta. But at least education has now become a major concern of the mass media, and coverage of education news improves steadily. Only a few publications are content to turn out consistently vapid and uncritical writing on education. In a word, the national press these days has an influence on education that is probably greater than ever before.

One could go on mentioning national groups of considerable variety that have some effect on education from time to time. There is, for example, the Committee for Economic Development, a group of two hundred leading people in business and education that has a subcommittee on education and often turns out policy statements on educational matters. There is the Chamber of Commerce, the Farm Bureau, the AFL-CIO, the National Association of Manufacturers, veterans organizations, and many more groups that take a fairly regular interest in educational policy and that can sometimes make their voice heard both on the national scene and through materials they distribute to the schools. There are also the special interest groups on the political right and left, and there are numerous civil rights organizations, that collectively and often singly can affect educational policy.

But perhaps we have said enough in this chapter to indicate how important national nongovernmental organizations are in the control of American education. When they are considered together with the federal government, they exercise a degree of power over education that makes nonsense of much of our talk about having a decentralized system.

STATE GOVERNMENT AND STATEWIDE GROUPS

Chapter IV

THE CONSTITUTIONS of all fifty states specifically assign basic responsibility for public education to the state. In many cases the state constitution spells out the government of education in extensive detail. Educational expenditures of state governments, though varying greatly, are in all cases a major consumer of taxes. In other words the fundamental unit of control in American education is supposed to be the state, although education seldom plays a role in state affairs that accords with these facts. The manner in which the states carry out their educational responsibilities remains a grave shortcoming in our educational politics.

The states have customarily been content to maintain within the apparatus of the state bureaucracy a department of education that is weak and ill-respected and that has often had, in its administration of state education policies, a deleterious effect on education. Many states too have allowed nongovernmental groups to assume an unconscionably large influence over education. There is perhaps no other function of state government that has received so little attention from the states in relation to the amounts of money involved.

But, as in so many other aspects of our educational system, the states are now beginning to change. They are being forced to reconsider their constitutional provisions for education and the role of state government in carrying them out. In this chapter we obviously cannot survey in any detail the individual states and the manner in which they run their educational affairs. We must settle for trying to delineate general trends and for looking at illustrative examples, recognizing that variation in details among the fifty states is as great in education as in anything else. I do not agree with a study done by one group of investigators a few years ago in which they found the variation in educational controls so great in the three midwestern states they examined as to lead them to think that a separate study of each state would be needed before "meaningful comparisons and generalizations" could be made.[1] Many such comparisons and generalizations, I am sure, can be made on the basis of present knowledge. But I would add that we have had very little formal study of state politics and education; and it would be foolish to pretend that we can do more here than sketch in a broad-brush outline of how education is governed at the state level. But such an outline is important to our purposes.

State Legislatures

In theory, the seat of educational power in every state is the legislature. In practice, state legislatures have failed with great frequency to exercise this power. When they have exercised it, they have often done so badly. The problem grows in part out of our governmental structure, which gives "low visibility" to legislators at the state level. They are part timers whose main business is not lawmaking. They are poorly paid. They generally have no staff. Not many first-rate people are attracted to the ranks. And state legislators often operate under outmoded, agrarian constitutions, some of which are exceedingly long and prescriptive.

But most of all, state legislators find that education is not an issue that gives them much political leverage. Individual legislators, that is, do not find that pushing particular educational reforms gets them many votes. They may be forced regularly to respond and support the professional education lobby—that is incontestably the case in a great many of the state legislatures—or they may be forced to support individual lobbyists such as state college presidents, but they have not been forced or encouraged by the laymen of their constituency to develop real insight into educational issues or to mount any educational crusades. This legislative apathy may owe something also to what many people would call the malapportionment of the legislature, with the rural areas overrepresented and oversupported at the expense of the cities. It is still too soon to know the detailed effects of the Supreme Court's first reapportionment decision in 1962, and of later decisions expanding it, but the consequences for education are bound to be considerable. Both the cities and the suburbs, particularly the latter, are going to have a far greater representation than in the past, and this fact would seem to mean greater pressures of many kinds for state legislators, and it may mean a more active, not to say aggressive, legislature in educational matters.

One of the ways in which this increased legislative interest will probably be expressed is in returning to the state government some of the control traditionally extended by the states to local government. Hawaii has created a single system of education, and the several constitutional conventions that have been held in the states since World War II have all reexamined the structure of educational control in order to increase the state's role. In the same way that Congress has increasingly claimed authority in education, state legislatures will probably reclaim some of their authority from the local districts. Even so, I would not stress this shift in legislative attitudes, with or without reapportionment. Most of the state legislatures will continue to be marked by a great deal of lethargy toward education, except as it relates to issues like desegregation and financial aid to local school systems.

California, however, is one state in which the legislature is notable for its activity in education and its broad interest in educational policy. Until the 1960's the record of the California legislature was not significantly different in education from that of other states, but the population influx reached such proportions in the present decade and made such financial demands on the state, especially in education, which consumes over half the state budget, that both the legislature and the governor's office began to show a special interest in how all the money was being spent. So of course did the general public, especially after Sputnik. One of the things the governor did was to appoint people to the state board of education who would not be merely a rubber stamp for the state superintendent. One of the things the legislature did was to create in 1961 a special full-time staff for the education committee of the assembly (the lower house), which was fortunate in getting a particularly able man as its chief analyst. The result was a remarkable improvement in the educational analyses and advice available to state legislators. They no longer had to depend for these critical services on lobbies or on state agencies that they had grown to distrust.

Thus the period between 1961 and 1967 became one in which the California legislature was more involved in education than the legislature of any other state. Among the many pieces of legislation debated and passed during this period was the well known Fisher Act, which embodied a thorough reform of state requirements for the licensing of teachers and administrators. Other major legislation concerned school redistricting, the measurement of student achievement, and the teaching of reading and foreign languages.

Some people would say that the legislature in California has become too active in education and that it has been overly specific in its legislation. If true, the legislature has only been reacting to the failure of the state department of education and other bodies to insure a level of educational quality appropriate to the expenditures. It has also been reacting to the long history of domination of the legislature by the educational establishment in California and the doubts felt by many legislators about the data given them by such bodies as the California Teachers Association. I feel myself that the legislature's work of the last seven years has done far more good than harm and that other legislatures might well look to their record.

Fortunately, the present trend in state legislatures seems to be toward the creation of full-time research staffs. Most of them now have some kind of legislative council to provide independent research and information to the legislature, though few states have yet created a staff office devoted solely to education. It may be that the new Education Commission of the States will be able in the future to see that state politicians are better informed on educational issues than they now are. I will discuss this organization, which grew out of a suggestion of James Bryant Conant for an "Interstate Compact for Education," in the last chapter. Suffice it here to say that the Education Commission has an unparalleled opportunity to strengthen the government of education within the states. But at the moment, education is still not a "gut" issue in most state houses, and campaigning for its improvement does not garner many votes. Until it does, state education policy will continue to be made outside most of the state legislatures.

State Boards of Education

The state-level administration of education is customarily carried out through a triumvirate made up of the state board of education, the state superintendent of education, and the state department of education. The duties of each in theory and in practice, and the ways in which people are brought to serve in these positions, differ extremely among the states. Some boards are elected, some appointed by the governor, and some are constituted *ex officio;* some have as few as three or five members, some over twenty; some members serve for only two years, some for thirteen; some boards meet every week, some only once a quarter. Some state superintendents are elected, some appointed by the governor, and some are appointed by the state board; some serve only one or two years, some six; some are *ex officio* members of the board of education, some not; some are responsible to the board of education, some not. Some state departments of education are large in relation to population, some are tiny; some are well supported, some are impoverished; some are weak, some are weaker.

In spite of the claims of professional educators and others for the superiority of one method or another of staffing these state offices, there is really no evidence to indicate that the selection, for instance, of a state board by the governor is better than selection by popular vote, or that the selection of a state superintendent is better done by the state board than by the electorate. As in most government posts, if good people run for election, education in the state will be better off than if second-rate persons are appointed by the governor or somebody else—and vice versa. The customary recommendation of professional educators is that state boards should be popularly elected on a nonpartisan ballot (a system now used in ten states and in prospect in others), and that the board should then appoint the superintendent to run the department of education and serve at the board's pleasure. It is as good a way as any but not clearly better than others.

The administration of education by the states is now beginning for the first time to receive some concerted study, mostly as a result of federal activity in education and the resulting desire of many people to see the hand of the states strengthened. There seems to have been a widespread discovery recently that state boards, state superintendencies, and state departments are frequently manned by undistinguished persons whose abilities leave a good deal to be desired. One of the main arguments offered by people who support the "categorical" approach to federal aid, including some professional educators, is that the states are not yet competent to spend unrestricted federal funds and cannot be trusted with them. This was the position taken, for example, by John H. Fischer, president of Teachers College (Columbia University), in a minority statement attached to a 1967 report of NEA's Educational Policies Commission; and also by another professional educator, Richard I. Miller, who concluded, after a lengthy study sponsored by the Office of Education, that a few states might do a good job if federal funds were given them with no strings attached, but that "the vast majority would fumble the ball in terms of professional leadership, political forces, and departmental pressures . . ." [2]

The state board of education acts both as the executive arm of the legislature and as a legislature in its own right. It must, that is, carry out educational legislation but is usually left a wide margin of discretion in which to make its own policies. For example, the legislature may pass a law outlining the general requirements for the licensing of teachers but may leave it to the state board to interpret the law and specify the requirements in detail. The state board may also govern textbook selection in the schools of the state, may act as a court of appeals in disputes, may define racial imbalance and enforce desegregation, may establish the length of the school day and year, may create statewide testing programs, may direct the preparation of statewide syllabuses or courses of study, may itself run special educational institutions, may oversee the consolidation or reorganization of school districts, and may adopt policies directly affecting standards and the curriculum.

In a word, the state board may do nearly anything it likes within the state's laws to control education. But it rarely governs in any but the most general way. Either it allows the state department of education to make many policies, an unfortunate but frequent occurrence, or it yields a great deal of its power to local school authorities. Southern state boards are apt to be more domineering than northern, but all are permissive.

For example, most of the states do not attempt to mandate the school curriculum to any great extent, certainly not to the extent that complaining educators might lead one to think. A survey of state curricular requirements in 1966 indicated that the great majority of the states mandate instruction in the dangers of alcohol and narcotics, that only a little over half of them require work in United States history, that half require physical education, and that less than half—ranging from 46 percent down to 2 percent of the states—require instruction in other specific subjects. Although some states (Iowa, California, and Indiana) have over thirty "curriculum prescriptions," over half the states have fewer than ten.[3] In other words, neither the state legislatures nor the state boards of education in most cases attempt to stipulate anything like a full school curriculum even though their power to do so is clear.

Even in matters where the state board has enunciated specific educational policies, enforcement is a wholly different matter. The fact is that there are few policies that cannot be circumvented by local districts with a real desire to do so. Lack of enforcement of established policies of the state board is therefore a major problem in most states, though I must add that this frequent non-compliance on the part of local districts is not always and necessarily bad. If the state board's policies are themselves bad, perhaps we should be grateful that they are not enforced.

Membership on state boards follows no particular patterns. The 480 men and women currently serving on state boards of education comprehend all manner of occupations and backgrounds, without any major differences discernible between members who are elected and those appointed. A majority of them belong to the National Association of State Boards of Education, a relatively new organization that is not known very widely but that has a good deal of potential influence. Some state boards are also members of the state association of local school boards but are not very active in them and are not encouraged to be.

The state superintendent of education, known among educators as the "chief state school officer," is almost always a member in good standing of the professional establishment. If he were not an orthodox professional educator, he would stand a poor chance of either election or appointment. There is the occasional exception, such as the election of Max Rafferty, a professional educator but not one of whom the establishment is fond, to the superintendency in California in 1962. Although the state superintendent may have a good deal of authority and may run a large bureaucracy, his pay and prestige are low, with the result that state superintendents are rarely prominent figures either in education or public affairs. If you were to ask any random sample of scholars, professional educators, or knowledgeable laymen to name the leading twenty-five or fifty educators in the country, the names of state superintendents would be conspicuously absent. Yet they are the persons who execute the policies of what are supposed to be the principal bodies in control of our educational system.

How much power the superintendent actually wields depends on many factors. If a state superintendent has a weak board that he can dominate, he will be able to exercise a great deal of authority; if he has a strong board, he may be limited. If the state has a highly prescriptive constitution or an active legislature, his freedom of action may also be limited. Many superintendents naturally find themselves somewhere in between, but in the nature of things they most often are able to exert a substantial influence over state policy. One therefore hopes that the important post of state superintendent will be filled in the future by abler people than has generally been the case in the past.

All state superintendents belong to a national organization called the Council of Chief State School Officers, headquartered in Washington. Its main job is to keep its members informed about federal legislation relevant to state departments of education, to act as a clearing house of information, and to be the general means of intercommunication for state superintendents. It also acts as a lobby and devotes considerable effort to "educating" members of Congress and other Washington officials. The CCSSO likes to think of itself as an independent voice, at least independent of the establishment, even though it accepts free office space from the NEA, but in fact it is a natural part of the establishment and is rarely found in opposition to NEA policies.

Interestingly enough our two most populous states, New York and California, illustrate something of the difference that exists in the relationships of the state boards to their chief executives. New York's legislature is relatively inactive in education and rarely legislates with much specificity in school matters. A notable exception to this rule occurred in 1967 when the New York legislature, against the advice of the Board of Regents and the State Education Department, demanded from the mayor of New York City a decentralization plan for the city's schools as a condition to giving him extra state aid, but this action may have been more a reflection of the legislature's unease over social and racial questions in New York City than over the quality of the schools. Generally the legislature in New York has been content to leave the governing of education to other people; namely the State Board of Regents (New York has no state board of education as such) and the state commissioner of education.

The New York Board of Regents was established in the Revolutionary era. Its members are elected by the state legislature for thirteen-year terms, and they in turn elect the commissioner of education to serve at their pleasure. The New York regents probably exercise more control over all aspects of education, including the only statewide system of school-leaving examinations in the country, than does the board of education of any other state. They in turn relinquish to the commissioner, who is their chief executive officer and directly responsible to them, more authority over educational policy and practice than most state superintendents enjoy, and he executes his responsibilities through the largest and best financed state department of education in the country. In short, the state control of education in New York is unique. It has been refined over a long period of time and the lines of responsibility are clearly drawn. With some reservations, particularly with regard to New York City, the State Education Department is generally recognized as more effective perhaps than any other.

In California the legislature, as we have seen, has become quite active in education. It not only involves itself in major policy questions but, thanks to a state "Education Code" that is extremely detailed and restrictive, it must regularly pass large numbers of purely routine education bills. The California state board is appointed by the governor for staggered terms of four years. He can appoint half the board in a two-year period and a majority in three. The board enjoys extensive authority, though much less than the New York Board of Regents. It does not appoint the state superintendent, who is a constitutional officer in California and elected by the public on a nonpartisan ballot. He is the executive officer of the state board but is not answerable to it, or to anybody else except the electorate.

Thus the execution of the board's policies can be and frequently is a highly uncertain business. The board can order the superintendent to support a particular bill before the legislature, but he can simply decline to do so; or he can do so badly or send somebody else to do so badly. The board can ask the superintendent to gather information essential to the formation of policy but he is not obligated to do so; nor can the board be certain that the policies it does adopt will be carried out by the superintendent. The board frequently finds itself, therefore, going around the superintendent directly to subordinates in the department of education or to outsiders for advice and help.

Professional educators commonly deplore the California situation, though they were not vocal about it before the election of Rafferty, and there undeniably are frustrations and inefficiencies built into the existing situation. If the governor fails to appoint members to the board who are in reasonable harmony with the superintendent, or the public elects a superintendent who is anathema to the board, one has a formula for trouble, particularly when the superintendent is not legally responsible to the board.

The California legislature itself, if one is to judge by a committee report in 1967, has grown tired of the armed combat between the present board and the superintendent, and wants to move toward a system similar to New York's whereby the legislature would elect the state board from a group of names submitted by the governor and the board would appoint the superintendent. In regard to the present situation, the committee said bluntly that

> Educational administration in this state, as it exists in Sacramento, consists of a chaotic, unplanned collection of boards, agencies, commissions and officers, connected sometimes by dotted lines of authority and sometimes by no lines at all. It resembles nothing so much as a blunderbuss approach to satisfying the pinpointed and crucial needs of public education in the nation's most populous state . . . as an elected state official, the superintendent has a right and, indeed, a duty to speak out on educational issues of the day. When he does so—and his views conflict sharply with those

of the Board of Education—misunderstandings and eventual harm to education are bound to ensue. Obviously, such instances have occurred during the past four years. This committee has no desire to become embroiled in the controversies which have raged between the Superintendent of Public Instruction and the State Board of Education during this period, nor will we take sides. But we do condemn the harmful effects of such frankly partisan battles on our state's public school system. We are convinced that our state-level educational structure fosters such unfortunate occurrences.[4]

Although the New York system and that of other states may work more smoothly than California's, I would not condemn the latter out of hand. There is much to be said for an active legislative involvement in education, and something to be said for elected superintendents. After all, education in California went through one of its worst periods under a state superintendent who began as a governor's appointment and who operated in great harmony with a board of education that was a rubber stamp. In 1945 Governor Earl Warren appointed Roy Simpson to fill out the unexpired term of the state superintendent, who had died. Simpson, a man of no particular distinction in education, was a purely political appointment. He was approved by what one investigator calls "a member of the inner group of prestige superintendents" who remarked on one occasion: " 'Simpson's never done anything to anyone, and he belongs to the [Masonic] lodge, so why not put him in?' "[5] Warren did put him in and gave California what might most charitably be called an era of lackluster leadership in education.

The California situation could no doubt be improved and will be when the board and the superintendent are in closer harmony, as is now happening. (By February 1968 Governor Reagan had appointed six out of the ten state board members, thus giving himself and Rafferty what might be called an ideological majority.) But it may well be that the net effect of California's seemingly chaotic manner of governing education will turn out to be better than that of many other states that have no system of checks and balances in their educational machinery. In addition, California's strong state board and flamboyant superintendent have heightened public interest in education to a degree never before realized.

State Departments of Education

As I have already indicated, the agencies maintained by the states within their own governmental structure to carry out the educational policies of the legislature and the board of education have characteristically been weak and ineffective. These agencies are usually called state departments of education and are supposed to supply educational leadership for the state, as well as to keep the legislature educationally informed, act as inspectors of schools, dispensers of aid, licensers of teachers, and a source of expert guidance in general to local school systems. They also have supervisory responsibilities in certain aspects of higher education, vocational education, adult education, and assorted other fields.

State departments range from large bureaucracies in such a state as New York where the State Education Department rivals in size the central ministries of education in England and Europe, to small and insignificant offices in states like Wyoming and the Dakotas. Their size, however, is not always proportional to the population: California with 20 million people has a state department of about two thousand employees and an administrative budget of under $20,000,000; Massachusetts with a quarter of California's population has a state department almost as big and an administrative budget of over $25,000,000.

But whatever their size and powers, almost without exception they are ill-equipped to carry out their duties, and they command no great respect from the school systems of their states. They are usually handicapped with line-item budgets and rigid civil service procedures for personnel. They may be able to wield a good deal of authority but only in ways approved by the rest of the establishment. Most people, including most professional educators, would agree that the state departments have been better in "pushing from the rear than in marching boldly out in front."

They have been better at policing, that is, than leadership. In my opinion they have not done either job well. An insider of long experience puts the matter this way:

> Many states . . . are still poorly equipped to perform the vital role which they must assume in education. Few states, for example, have a state board with prestige, the caliber of lay members, or the broad responsibility, overall, of education that their responsibilities call for. Some state departments are poorly staffed, too highly bureaucratized, and politically dominated. Some are characterized by intellectual incest: All personnel, in training and experience, seem to have come from the state's own educational system. Their qualifications show little outbreeding with business and industry, subject matter disciplines, and diversified provenance. Budgets are usually inadequate, and restrictions in expenditure make even available funds difficult to use effectively. . . . In the face of these conditions, state education departments have been flooded with new administrative responsibilities for Federal programs. They find themselves with more money than talent.[6]

This view puts the state departments in a better light than they probably deserve, for many of their failings are due to circumstances quite within their control. James Bryant Conant is much blunter and more accurate in the following assessment:

> The major weakness of all the state departments of education I have encountered, with perhaps one or two exceptions, is that they are too much a part of the educational establishment. That is, I found many of these agencies, unlike the regulatory commissions at the Federal level, to be little more than the "willing tools" of the interests and clientele, particularly the education association [that is, the NEA state affiliate]. In more than one state I heard highly placed education and political officials claim that state departments of education "follow a party line" or "reflect the public school mentality." These terms were used in a derogatory sense. A grave shortcoming of our educational leadership at the state level, in my opinion, is often its unwillingness or

incapacity to respond to forces outside the establishment. These agencies seldom solicit the opinions of educational experts or critics who are not associated with public schools or professional education, and in those rare instances when they do ask the advice of "outside" experts, I suspect it is largely for symbolic purposes. Too often, educational leadership at the state level—official and unofficial—has been open to the charge that it was unwilling to examine public school needs critically.[7]

Considering Conant's usual restraint in criticizing the American professional educator, this evaluation of state departments is all the more cogent.

In fact, there has been very little formal study of state departments, very few histories of them, and no comprehensive critiques. In view of their powers, they have been surprisingly neglected in professional studies. Now, however, there is an upsurge of interest in them as a result of the many federal aid programs that are being administered by them. These programs consume an astonishing amount of the time of their professional staffs— one study found that "more than 70 per cent of the full-time staff [in 1966] were paid in whole or in part by Federal funds." [8] Title V of the Elementary and Secondary Education Act of 1965 also provides more money than has ever been available before for the study and reform of state departments. Title V is quite unprecedented in our history: direct grants to the states for the specific purpose of improving their departments of education. So far no state, however strong may be its devotion to states' rights, has turned down this kind of federal "intervention." Title V funds have been used in a wide variety of ways. They have financed, for example, a full-scale study of the California state department by an industrial consulting firm, whose report found the department poorly organized in dealing with its responsibilities, too rigid, compartmentalized, uncoordinated, and haphazard.[9] Multistate studies have also been invited by the Office of Education, and at least two are nearing completion with Title V funds and another dozen are in various stages of operation.

Practically all of the state departments have now organized self-studies of one sort or another, often a dozen or more of them, under Title V money, but with what success remains to be seen. One suspects that self-studies are hardly what is needed in view of the past failures of state departments. Again, it is California's state board that has been more vigorous than others in the use of Title V funds. It has avoided self-assessments by the California State Department of Education, feeling that the weaknesses of the department were the reason for undertaking Title V studies in the first place.

The Office of Education has also created a nationwide historical study of state departments, being done by the Council of Chief State School Officers. Early in the study the council decided that the only feasible way in which to get the main part of the job done was to ask each state department to write a history of itself and submit it for inclusion in a projected volume of histories. It seems safe to predict that these half a hundred separate histories will be as uneven in quality as they are sympathetic to the departments; commissioned histories rarely exhibit independence of mind.

There is also to be a second volume, on special topics such as teacher certification, curriculum control, and "Leadership and Coordination to Achieve Suitable Scope and Quality in Education." If we are to judge by the number of old establishment hands who have been hired to do the writing, both volumes have every prospect of being an elaborate and expensive apologia. But I suppose that even if they are, they will bring together more information about state departments of education than has been available before in one place.

In the meantime what we can say is that state departments in the main continue to perform worst at their most important functions. In licensing teachers and administrators they are as rigid as they ever were; in the inspection of schools they either ignore their responsibilities entirely or impose a set of mechanical criteria of dubious validity; in research and data gathering they are simply and consistently inadequate; in operating educational establishments of their own they are without any kind of distinction in a job in which they of all agencies should excel; and in long-range planning for the state and in providing strong educational leadership they are failures—if one tries to think of a major educational reform of the last quarter of a century that has come about through a state department of education, one is faced with a formidable task.

What are the chances of improvement now that much more attention and money are being given state departments than ever before? Fair in some things, dim in others. Much depends on whether state government in general can be improved at the same time, for it is probably fallacious to assume that state education departments can be reformed in a vacuum. Despite the fact that they tend to be isolated in the state machinery and have little contact with other bureaus, which is one of their problems, they do have to operate at the salary levels and in the whole context of the rest of state government, and so cannot move very far in advance of other departments.

State government in general, if we are to believe Terry Sanford, the noted former governor of North Carolina, has a history of inactivity, corruption, and timidity. Sanford has expressed himself in many places on what he calls our "moribund" state governments. To his fellow governors he likes to say things like, "Some who have argued loudest and shrillest for states rights, have done more to undermine states rights [through incompetence and inactivity] than anyone else in the union." [10] In 1967 he completed a two-year study of state governments and in his report spells out their failings in great detail, especially their failings in urban education and urban affairs in general.[11] If his diagnosis is correct, the whole of state government must be renovated if the state departments of education are to be genuinely improved.

Voluntary Statewide Agencies and Groups

Of the many nongovernmental organizations that attempt to influence public policy, only one or two are consistently important in education at the state level. The most important is the state teachers association; that is, the state NEA affiliate. As yet the AFT is not strong at the state level and is a significant force in state politics only on rare occasions in northern states that have AFT chapters in large cities.

Affiliates of the NEA flourish in all the states and have a much larger proportional membership than does the national NEA. The great majority of classroom teachers belong to their local and state NEA, but only a shade over half of them belong to the national body. Even so the pattern is uneven. A far lower percentage of teachers in the northeastern states, where the NEA is relatively unimportant, join the state affiliate than teachers in the Midwest, for example, where the NEA is powerful. Thus the state affiliates differ greatly in the amount of political pressure they can exert. Moreover, many teachers also belong to more than one teachers organization. Dual membership in the NEA and AFT is not unusual.

In states where the NEA has high memberships, such as Iowa or Kansas or Illinois, the state affiliate is indeed one of the largest and most vocal professional pressure groups. It typically is headquartered in the capital city and its executives spend a great deal of their time pressuring the state department of education and lobbying in the state legislature. When the occasion demands it, the associations can flood state legislators with letters and telegrams from the teachers of their constituencies, and that can seem a threat to many a politician and state administrator who has not learned how to evaluate pressure. One investigation of how educational decisions get made at the state level found, not surprisingly, that

> The groups and individuals who articulate the policy proposals, the innovators so to speak, are those who have a direct and tangible stake in the outcome of the decisions . . . in each of the states we surveyed the major group was the state affiliate of the National Education Association; namely, the MSTA in Missouri, the IEA in Illinois, and the MEA in Michigan. These groups have a relatively high degree of or-

ganization, a principal spokesman, a wealth of information about school needs, and generally favorable access to at least some points in the *formal* decision-making structure.[12]

Like the national NEA, the state affiliates prefer to be known as something else besides political action groups, but that remains the most appropriate definition for many of them. They do other things besides talk to politicians, of course, as do all professional associations, but lobbying is perhaps their most important activity.

Unfortunately even experienced state legislators frequently have not learned to allow for the contrived nature of the pressure that the state NEA can exert. Nor do they appreciate the fact that teachers are often coerced by their administrators to join the state NEA and so are not necessarily sympathetic to its policies or a party to its politicking. I said something in Chapter II about the disagreeable habit of administrators of pressuring their teachers to join the national NEA, but it is probably even greater at the state level. The following conclusion from a recent study in Oregon, which is based on interviews with over eight hundred high school teachers in that state, seems to me equally applicable to many other states:

> The Oregon Education Association is old, well-established and influential. About three-quarters of the teachers in Oregon belong to it, and competition for the loyalties of teachers is practically non-existent. There is a teachers' union [an AFT affiliate], but very few teachers belong and it is not taken seriously by the leadership of the Oregon Education Association. In a very real sense, the OEA is the only organization available for teachers. Teachers join the Oregon Education Association, both because they think it will help them professionally and intellectually and because they believe that they are expected to join. Thirty-nine per cent of the teachers indicated that their primary motive in joining a professional association was to be exposed to professional literature and ideas, which they believed would lead to the improvement of teaching, raise the standards of the profession and make them better teachers. Twenty-one per cent

joined because they were requested to join or pressured to join by the administration. This persuasion was not necessarily overt, but these teachers believed that the smart thing to do was to join up. They were probably aware of the fact that, in the evaluation forms which are used in considerations of promotion and tenure, membership in professional organizations is a criterion. So, the Oregon Education Association is, to some extent, similar to a union in that its voluntary nature is somewhat compromised.[13]

Inasmuch as the above study was organized and conducted by professional educators under a grant from the United States Office of Education, one is tempted to suppose that it might put the best light on the situation. My own feeling is that coercion, overt and covert, plays an even greater role in NEA state membership revenues than is here suggested.

Occasionally a state affiliate will overplay its hand and bring itself into disrepute in the legislature or in the eyes of the public. For instance, the California Teachers Association, one of the most powerful of the NEA's state affiliates, mounted such a raucous and undignified campaign in 1962 to try to block the election of Max Rafferty as state superintendent as to undermine whatever confidence the public may have had in the CTA (prudently the CTA did not oppose Rafferty when he ran for reelection in 1964). Also the CTA, as we will see presently, lost the good will of many of the state's legislators a few years ago in its desperate efforts to block or emasculate a bill to reform the licensing of teachers and administrators in California.

Similarly, the Florida Education Association did not exactly endear itself to the state legislature when in 1966 the FEA sent each of its 50,000 members a questionnaire asking them to report to the FEA whatever they knew about the drinking or gambling habits, favorite restaurants, marital status, jail records, political supporters and contributors, and business clients of individual state legislators. When this questionnaire became public, as was inevitable the FEA came up with an explanation that was at least picturesque: the only reason, it seems, that the FEA wanted this information in confidence was to inform its staff about what to avoid in conversations with legislators!

Nevertheless state affiliates meet with success in their relations with the legislature far more often than with failure, even when they engage in unlawful "work stoppages." As I mentioned in Chapter II, the state affiliates in Oklahoma and Utah, with the help of the national NEA, invoked statewide strikes and threats of strikes in recent years and forced concessions from the governors and legislatures. The Florida Education Association in 1967 and 1968 fought a running battle with the governor and legislature. The FEA delivered an ultimatum in the fall of 1967 to the governor to call the legislature into session and vote increased school funds or face a strike. The governor was adamant for some weeks, declaring the real issue was not money but a question of whether the public was to be bludgeoned into compliance by the company union of the educational establishment; the FEA was equally adamant, declaring that the issue was "quality education." Ultimately the legislature offered to meet some of the FEA's demands but not all. In February 1968 the FEA finally carried out its threat to strike by "activating" signed but undated resignations from its members. An uncertain settlement was reached within a few weeks that did not represent a clear victory for either side.

But in still other states the NEA affiliate has little or no political leverage. It is not large enough in some states to be effective or it lacks vigorous leadership or is overshadowed by other lobbies. In those states where it is weak, one of its main failings is its lack of contact with the governor, in whose office the budget is constructed. And of course in those few states where the AFT is powerful in the cities, it can run the NEA competition that will become severe in the future. But the general picture is that the NEA's state affiliates are prime movers in state politics.

A second organization that is sometimes important is the state affiliate of the National School Boards Association. The national NSBA office is in Evanston, Illinois (though a Washington office was added in 1966), from whence it organizes conferences, supplies speakers, publishes and distributes to the states a large volume of educational literature. Its influence nationally is limited by its heterogeneity and the difficulty of its adopting policies that really represent a consensus of its state affiliates. It has problems, that is, of consensus that the teacher organizations don't have to worry about. Thus the national office is apt to shun controversy and promote only those policies that are in the obvious interests of school boards, such as the importance of maintaining lay control of education. It promotes such slogans as: "Local Control, State Responsibility, Federal Concern."

Unlike the NEA, the National School Boards Association is really a federation of state groups which in turn are federations of local school boards within the states. Almost all local school boards except the tiny ones belong to their state association, though most of them are not very active. Probably 90 percent of local school board members are represented in the state associations. Local boards are assessed dues on the basis of the number of teachers or students in the schools under their control, or sometimes on the basis of assessed valuation or total school expenditures. The state associations together take in about $3,000,000 a year, pale in comparison to the NEA, and most maintain a small full-time staff. Unfortunately, too many of them, like the national office, hire professional educators rather than laymen for their staff.

Production and distribution of educational literature is a major activity of all the state school board associations. They publish handbooks of data on school boards, most have a regular journal or newsletter, and all have occasional publications. Almost all of them have legislative committees that in theory look after school board interests in state government, but these committees are often inactive. When the state associations do lobby, they suffer from the same disability as the national office—the lack of a policy that is acceptable to and backed by their diverse membership—or sometimes by the fact that they are dominated by board members from rural elementary school districts. State associations often find themselves pitted in the legislative halls against the state board of education over such issues as local control and school district reorganization and are often bested. In general, the state school boards associations are not able to exert an influence comparable to the teachers association or, for that matter, to the state departments of education. However, if they ever decide to undertake an aggressive campaign and are able to hammer out a common policy, they could become a major force within the states.

Other state organizations are important in education only on occasion. The National Congress of Parents and Teachers, which I will discuss in the next chapter, has a state structure just as do the teachers organizations and the school boards, but rarely has any influence on state policy. State taxpayers' associations can sometimes have a substantial effect on educational expenditures. Unofficial citizens committees on rare occasions can also be effective in state legislatures.

Associations of teachers of special subjects can be surprisingly effective at the state level. Vocational education teachers, for example, must be considered a major force in many states. They are well financed and organized, and strongly unified in the protection of what they conceive to be their interests. The same is frequently true of physical education teachers and home economics teachers, backed by the manufacturers of sports equipment and home appliances. Such special groups, often acting through the NEA state affiliate, can bring a lot of pressure to bear on legislators and state boards of education on behalf of their specialties in the schools.

Ironically, the teachers of academic subjects are almost never a force of any consequence. They are poorly organized and led and are anything but unified. They and their professional associations seem to be the last groups that anybody at the state level thinks to consult on an educational question; and if they were consulted they probably would have few if any considered recommendations to offer. One has only to look at the state licensing requirements for teachers of nonacademic subjects and for those of academic subjects to realize whose voice is politically important. In most states an individual can be licensed to teach physics or mathematics or history with much less professional training in those subjects than he can be to teach home economics or industrial arts.

Efforts to reverse or change this grotesque situation are rarely successful. Illinois furnishes a current illustration: there a few years ago a group of scholars and laymen well known in the state formed an organization to try to reform the Illinois certification laws for teachers. It was called the Illinois Citizens' Committee for Teacher Education and it was led by the chairmen of several of the academic departments at Northern Illinois University, a former teachers college. Helped by a number of the state's outstanding academics, the committee between 1965 and 1968 tried to get some changes made or at least discussed in teacher certification of the kind recommended by James Bryant Conant and others over the last few years. Mostly the committee wanted a reduction of course requirements in pedagogy and education and an increase of requirements in academic study for teachers—a goal that practically everybody shares today except some professors of education.

But the professional establishment is powerful in Illinois. It did not look kindly on this committee that seemed to threaten its interests. And to date it has fought the committee with complete effectiveness; Illinois certification laws remain as lopsided as ever they were. Thus the teachers of academic subjects in our schools and colleges, a group that represents a majority of secondary and college teachers in every state, regularly loses the enormous influence that is potentially theirs to the professional establishment and to the vocational-education–physical-education–home-economics lobby; a curious phenomenon.

Nongovernmental organizations, then, are extremely various in their ability to influence state policy in education. By far the most important is the NEA state affiliate, though it can be countered by other groups when a crisis arises or when it pushes so hard as to disenchant people in the legislative and executive branches. But the fact remains that the academic community of any state—teachers of the academic subjects in the schools, members of the arts and sciences departments of the colleges—has little to say in the formation of state policies that directly affect them.

State Advisory Commissions

Although not a formal part of the state structure of education, special investigating commissions appointed from time to time by state governments can have an extremely important influence within the state and sometimes within the nation. Such bodies are, of course, a device frequently invoked by state politicians for doing nothing while seeming to do much; but when the reports of special commissions are taken seriously by the legislature, they can have lasting effects on education. Two examples from states widely separated geographically and in a great many other ways may serve to illustrate the role that state commissions can play in the politics of our educational system. California and Massachusetts have had reports by statewide investigating bodies in recent years and both have acted on the reports.

In the aftermath of Sputnik, public debate about the quality of American education set new decibel levels in many states. California was one of them, where both houses of the legislature voted unanimously in the winter of 1958 to create a Joint Interim Committee on the Public Education System. Its mandate was to examine and assess the California schools, which a lot of people were saying were expensive but inferior. The legislature further created a Citizens Advisory Commission to assist the Joint Interim Committee, and its members were chosen from what one legislator called the "most representative, talented and conscientious group of people ever gathered on one citizens' commission." [14]

The citizens commission worked for nearly two years, traveled throughout the state, took testimony from hundreds of witnesses, accumulated five thousand pages of evidence and documentation, and deliberated at length. There were many internal conflicts, especially between representatives of the educational establishment and the lay members of the commission. Not all of these conflicts were resolvable, so that the final majority report was accompanied by several minority statements, one of them a lengthy and detailed report in itself. Without reviewing the details of the work of this important commission, let me simply indicate the impact of its report.

The majority report made recommendations for fundamental reforms in (1) the training and licensing of teachers; (2) the elementary and secondary school curriculum; (3) the evaluation and selection of textbooks; (4) statewide testing programs; and (5) administrative procedures. Most of its recommendations were put into effect in succeeding years and have changed education in California in a number of critical ways.

Take teacher training, for example. The commission's recommendations for the preparation and licensing of teachers led to the introduction of the famed Fisher Bill into the California legislature in 1961. The battle-scarred voyage of this bill through the senate and the assembly is an instructive study in itself of the politics of American education, with the California establishment fighting the major provisions of the bill in all the ways it knew how but ultimately being beaten by strong press and gubernatorial support, by equally strong support from the state board of education, by a legislature weary of establishment tactics, and by the sheer weight of public opinion. When the Fisher Bill finally passed in a weakened but not crippled condition, it marked the first time in modern California history that the professional education lobby has not been able to block a major bill of which it disapproved.

The result was a reform in one of the most important areas of the state's educational system. Secondary school teachers in California now must be better educated than before and must have more work in the subjects they teach. Elementary school teachers must have a major in something besides education in college. Equally important, school administrators must be reasonably well educated persons who have some significant teaching experience, thus blocking the way to important administrative posts for physical education teachers, home economics teachers, and others. These seemingly modest improvements are actually quite radical, which was the reason for the bitter-end fight against them by such bodies as the California Teachers Association and the California Council on Teacher Education (a coalition of professional interest groups).

Opposition from the establishment continues today and is even regrouping for a counterattack in the legislature, hoping to rescind the Fisher Act. Particularly galling to the California establishment is the requirement that administrators have an academic background. Because of this opposition it has still not been possible for the state to carry out all the provisions of the Fisher Act and of its subsequent interpretations by the state board of education. Also, there are some indications, though far from clear, that the new requirements for elementary teachers may discourage some young women from entering training programs or encourage them to enter programs for secondary school teaching, which are not significantly tougher than elementary programs under the new rules. The California establishment likes to say that the Fisher Act has thus contributed to a shortage of elementary teachers (which is a general, not just a California, problem) and this was also one of the highly tentative findings of a study commissioned recently by the state board.[15] In January 1967 a subcommittee of the California Assembly expressed itself in no uncertain terms on the failures of the state's professional educators to honor the mandate given them by the public in the Fisher Act:

> Seldom in the history of California has a public mandate of such a proportion, heavily supported by both parties, been subjected to so much bureaucratic frustration. We think it is incumbent on the State Department of Education and the persons responsible for teacher education to accept the public demand and do their duty.[16]

But the behavior of the California establishment in regard to the Fisher Act is not the immediate point. The point is that special state commissions can sometimes have a fundamental effect on educational policy and practice; California's admirable Citizens Advisory Commission is one such example.

The other example I would like to cite, even more instructive, is the Special Commission appointed in 1962 by the Massachusetts General Court (the state legislature). As in the case of California, the work and results of the Massachusetts commission would make a valuable study in itself in the politics of American education and I hope that someone will undertake such a study in the future. Here we can only take room to sketch in the political background and say something about the success and limitations of this extraordinary state commission; but we must do so in enough detail to indicate the significance of the commission's work.

The Special Commission was created against a backdrop of general neglect of public education, both lower and higher, in Massachusetts. The state has a very large number of independent schools and colleges and an extensive system of Roman Catholic institutions, and it has a legislature that reflects ethnic and religious interests, especially Irish and Italian. These interests have traditionally complemented those of Roman Catholic schools and some private school groups to oppose strong support from the state for public education. They have especially opposed anything beyond minimum support for public institutions of higher education, which Roman Catholics have regarded as Protestant establishments and the independent colleges as a competitive threat.

Something of a crisis developed in the affairs of the state's only public university, the University of Massachusetts, in mid-1959, when a bill to raise the pay of its faculty members was introduced into the legislature. The *Boston Globe,* a statewide newspaper, launched a campaign of support for the bill by publishing a series of articles in the summer of 1959 by two reporters, Ian Menzies and Ian Forman, the latter being the first full-time education reporter the *Globe* had ever had. The main theme of the series was that public higher education in the state had been starved in the interests of tax-exempt private institutions that charged high fees, and that a large segment of the taxpayers was being denied the kind of equality of opportunity in higher education that was available in most of the other states at low or modest cost.

The bill was killed by its most vociferous enemy, the then president of the Massachusetts Senate, an experienced and peremptory killer of bills; but this time his action backfired. A good deal of public and political support had crystallized around the *Globe* articles, and it was reinforced by the angry resignation of the university's president. With support from the governor, the bill was refiled and passed, not because the legislature really supported it but because the lawmakers were afraid to oppose it any longer. The passage of this bill proved to be a kind of watershed in public education in Massachusetts.

The *Globe* followed up its success by giving regular space to education news and by reporting it better than had been done before in the state. In the fall of 1961, the same team of reporters, Menzies and Forman, published a series of stinging articles on the state's public school system. Having reported education for several years in Massachusetts, they had both developed an acute sense of dissatisfaction with public education and in particular with the Massachusetts State Department of Education, which they found to be ineffective and poorly regarded by school districts throughout the state. They also found the state board of education too subservient to the state commissioner of education, and to his department of education, and without power to force improvements on local school districts.

Menzies and Forman gave their series the inflammatory title, "The Mess in Bay State Education" and took as their theme the following: "Public education in Massachusetts—from kindergarten to university—is being run today by uninformed executives, legislators and fiscal clerks in the State House." With that as an opener, they described in some detail the sad condition of Massachusetts public schools and suggested a number of reforms, some of which would not cost money (such as an overhaul of the state board of education).

The reaction within Massachusetts to "The Mess in Bay State Education" was dramatic testimony to the power that the press can sometimes have over our educational system. It soon became clear that the *Globe* articles were producing or at least uncovering a public consensus about the need for educational reform— reform that would put an end once and for all to what one columnist called the "patronage and provincialism" of public education in Massachusetts. There was also a small but important body of support for reform in the legislature. "But we were opposed, of course," Forman now recalls, "by many elements of what Dr. Conant called the 'educational establishment' because our articles disturbed much of the old order. Many educators, however, also supported us privately—they admitted, that is, that drastic changes were needed but were afraid to say so publicly."

Among the legislative leaders on the side of reform were two important figures: Maurice A. Donahue, then Majority Floor Leader in the Senate, and a former teacher, and Kevin B. Harrington, also a former teacher. Soon after the *Globe* articles appeared, Donahue filed a bill to create a special state commission with a mandate broader than any in the state's history—to investigate "The entire educational system from primary grades through college" with a view to

> elevating educational standards in the commonwealth, reorganizing the scope of the various educational boards and administrators of the commonwealth, revising and modernizing the organization and financial structure of schools and school systems, extending the facilities, curricula and educational goals of the schools and colleges of the commonwealth, and providing increased financial aid for education.

There had been dozens of statewide study groups in the past in Massachusetts but none with the scope and all-embracing mandate of this one, and none whose reports were not yellowing and long forgotten on library shelves. Nor had other states created such a commission in modern times, although a few states had created statewide commissions to examine one or another segment of the state's educational system; California was again outstanding in its state commission that produced its Master Plan for Higher Education.

The Donahue bill, with strong support from the governor (who wanted a new broad-based tax in the state and saw the education commission as a way of getting it), passed with unusual ease. Harrington was appointed chairman of the commission, an appointment that proved to be extremely fortunate. He had a genuine interest in, and a considerable knowledge of, education in the state and was convinced of the significance of the commission. He fought from the beginning to keep it free of politics and refused to load either the commission itself, consisting of ten legislators and eleven laymen and educators, or its staff with political appointments.

One of the commission's first jobs was to find a full-time director. After considerable screening of names and after being turned down by Arthur S. Adams, then president of the American Council on Education, the commission turned to Benjamin C. Willis, then superintendent of schools in Chicago. Willis agreed to direct the study on less than a full-time basis. This was one of the few big mistakes made by the commission, though not in the end as serious as it might have been without an able back-up staff on the commission. The Boston newspapers had a number of harsh things to say about the $32,000 to be paid Willis as salary and expenses in return for his spending his weekends in Massachusetts and his full time for one summer. The appointment also turned sour when Willis encountered serious trouble at home over school integration and, since Chicago was paying him the highest salary of any school administrator in the country, over his moonlighting in Massachusetts.

This unfavorable publicity got things off to a knotty start for the commission but did no permanent damage. The commission put together a good staff of eight people who worked well together for the better part of two years. With the exception of Willis and his first assistant, there were no establishment figures on the staff.

Once in operation the commission was left remarkably free of political pressure, and its twenty-one members soon shook down to a faithful, hard working group of about fifteen. As it proceeded, however, the commission found the job of developing a detailed master plan for all of public education in Massachusetts too big. For one thing they had to spend a lot of time and money gathering simple data of the kind that should have been available from the department of education. They decided to restrict themselves to what seemed to them the preeminent need: a reform of the state structure for governing public education, a reform that would allow other reforms to be made over time.

We cannot here examine the details of the commission's report, which appeared in 1965,[17] but we should note its main recommendations. It recommended the creation of a new state board of education composed wholly of laymen and with far greater power than the old. With the new board the commission hoped to accomplish a number of things. It hoped, for instance, to take the legislature out of the business of making detailed education laws; it hoped to return to the state some of the control over education that the old board had lost bit by bit to the local districts. (It proposed to do this by giving the new board power to withhold state aid from school districts that did not meet various guidelines and minimum standards to be established by the board.) It hoped to reduce the policy-making power of the commissioner of education, who dominated the old board; and it wanted to remove educational professionals from the board so as to reassert the primacy of lay control of educational policy.

The commission also recommended the creation of a state board of higher education to be responsible for basic policy and to coordinate the budgets and operations of all the state-supported institutions of higher education. It wanted, that is, a single public university with a number of branches. This board was also to be composed wholly of laymen, but was to include many of the laymen already serving as trustees of public institutions of higher education. (This was probably another mistake.)

The commission recommended the creation of still a third lay-controlled agency unlike anything to be found in the other states. It was an "Advisory Council on Education" and it was defended in this way by the commission:

> Currently there is no machinery for constant and continuous review of all public education in the Commonwealth except the General Court which has found it necessary to authorize over 100 studies of education in this century, 65 of them since World War II. It is no longer feasible for the Legislature of the Commonwealth to have to act as a school board for all public education in Massachusetts.
>
> The Commission recognizes the crucial need for continuing long-range evaluation, planning, and innovation. Thus a third lay board is proposed . . . [to] analyze and study the programs and systems used by all agencies for public education in the Commonwealth.

Another major recommendation of the commission was for a thorough reorganization of the State Department of Education. The commission wanted a consolidation of the department's fourteen divisions—"fourteen little empires," as one commission member commented—and a variety of other changes to improve the quality of the department and to give it some chance of earning the respect of local school districts. Still other recommendations covered such matters as curriculum and standards, teacher training, and school finance.

But the heart of the report were the proposals for creating three lay boards and reconstructing the education department; and it was these proposals that produced the hottest debates while the commission was sitting and later when a bill which had been prepared by the commission to carry out its recommendations was making its tortuous way through the legislature. The idea of the lay boards was firmly opposed by the commissioner of education, who fought for what he called the right of professional educators "to serve." But too many members of the commission feared that the professionals' service might be self-service and that their presence on the proposed boards would merely perpetuate the old ingrown system that the commission was seeking to replace.

Looking back on this lengthy fight, Kevin Harrington, now Majority Floor Leader of the Massachusetts Senate, recalls that as the commission went about its work it was so struck by the vehemence of the stand-patters and by the various pressures they sought to exert on the commission that the idea of the lay boards came naturally to the surface within the commission as an essential counter to the establishment.

The department of education put up one of the longest fights the commission experienced. The department's opposition was chiefly over the commission's recommendations for departmental reorganization and over what was thought to be a threatened reduction in senior positions. The campaign mounted by some of the department's division chiefs, especially in vocational education, is itself a classic example of lobbying techniques by the establishment. Vocational education, thanks to half a century of generous financing by the federal government, has now grown into a major segment of our educational system and constitutes a vested interest of formidable power. The influence it can bring to bear in many of our state legislatures is not to be taken lightly. The Massachusetts vocational education lobby fought the commission's bill down to the wire and very nearly won.

Other people also opposed the bill. Organized labor disliked it because of the greatly increased financial aid to schools that would be involved and which labor feared, quite rightly, would be raised by means of a state sales tax. Various institutions of higher education objected out of a fear of losing what they thought was their share of tax funds from the new board of higher education. The professional association representing teachers of retarded and handicapped children carried on an emotion-charged campaign against the bill on grounds that it would devalue their specialty. And the bill was not helped by the fact that, as it was being debated, Benjamin Willis, back in Chicago, was in deeper trouble than ever with his own board and constituency, and was being "allowed to retire."

But the commission also had important support. The League of Women Voters and other such groups made their voices heard on behalf of the commission's bill. The *Globe*'s Ian Forman, having been a principal force in causing the commission to be created in the first place, kept up a drumfire of support for its bill. His articles kept saying things like:

One question can legitimately be asked of anyone who is disturbed by the commission's proposal to put top policy-making in the hands of lay citizens: Namely, what would any professional educator have to fear from an intelligent prestigious board of lay people, drawn from all segments of Bay State society?

One might even say that the *Globe* was the most effective lobby of all in support of the commission's bill. Harrington and the senate's leadership were solidly behind the bill, of course. So were the governor and most of his party (Republican), for they saw it as a vehicle for getting through the legislature a sales tax with which to meet the costs involved, thereby avoiding an increase in income or other taxes.

Opponents of the bill finally defeated themselves. Toward the end of the debates when the bill was due to come up for a vote, the opponents got out what Harrington at the time called "one of the most viciously clever" pieces of propaganda he had ever seen. It was an unsigned pamphlet inserted into the mail box of each legislator in which a wholly distorted view of the bill, and especially of its costs, was put forward. The technical details of the pamphlet suggested that some establishment groups, strongly suspected to be in the state education department, had done the writing but had declined to sign their names. The Speaker of the Massachusetts House finally announced that he had had enough of the "special interests in the so-called educational establishment [that were] trying to cripple the bill by amendment. As Speaker, I do not intend to sit idly by while the outstanding work of the Harrington Commission is thoroughly emasculated."

The bill passed in June 1965 and Forman reported triumphantly in the *Globe*:

A new era in Massachusetts public education was assured Tuesday when the Senate passed the Willis-Harrington bill

—without major amendments—by an overwhelming 37 to 1 rollcall vote. The House has already approved the far-ranging measure and Governor Volpe's signature is a foregone conclusion since he—along with top Democratic leadership—has supported it from the beginning. The Senate's resounding bipartisan vote laid the groundwork for a revamping and improvement of Bay State public education from kindergarten to university. . . . The one-sided final tally was a tribute to Harrington.

But it is an open question whether a majority of the legislature, had they been able to vote secretly, would not have voted down the bill because it required new taxes. As subsequent events proved, the electorate was ahead of the legislature on both counts: on its enthusiasm for the commission's report and on its willingness to face new taxes to put the commission's recommendations into effect.

What, then, have been the measurable results of the work of this extraordinary state commission? Much less so far than its supporters hoped; much more than its opponents expected. It did not give Massachusetts a master plan for public education, but it did give the state the means for developing one. It did not come to grips in any specific way with such problems as racial imbalance, school district reorganization, vocational education, teacher certification (though it produced an excellent chapter on what is wrong with teacher education in Massachusetts), and other major problems; but it did identify problems that urgently needed action and it did give the state a body that could be held responsible for tackling such problems.

The new state board of education has not moved as vigorously as expected in setting and enforcing some kind of minimum educational standards throughout the state. Instead the board has been preoccupied with trying to enforce the state's strong and unique racial imbalance law, and in its first attempt to use the considerable teeth given it by the legislature—power to withhold state aid from school districts that do not meet the board's standards—ran afoul of the redoubtable Boston School Committee. The board did not, as many of its supporters in the press and legislature and among the public expected, find a new state commissioner of education. It kept the old one "for the sake of continuity," as one board member now observes with regret, feeling that the board thereby compromised what was to have been a brave new order in Bay State education.[18] The board has proved more timid in general than many people expected, but this body does have real power to reform the educational system and may be willing to use it in the future; meanwhile it is a great deal better than the old board.

Similarly the new board of higher education has not met expectations. It has had only limited success in trying to unify and coordinate the state-supported institutions of higher education. One problem has been that its members have been engaged in a good deal of infighting for position, with spokesmen for the various institutions struggling only on behalf of their part of the system of higher education—the very thing the board was set up to avoid. The board could not even moderate its jealousies enough to agree on a chancellor for the first year of its operation. But again these little power struggles will, one hopes, diminish in the future and the board, which is the first of its kind in the state's history, will be able to bring some rational planning and general supervision to the state's institutions of higher education.

So the commission's success has hardly been complete, in part because the governor failed to make enough outstanding appointments to the lay boards. He made a few excellent ones, some good ones, many fair ones. And he avoided making any purely political ones, thus establishing an important precedent for future governors. But he did not make enough appointments of the kind that are essential—men and women of real prestige, dedication, and ability—if the promise of the commission's report is to be realized. Even so the creation of these boards has radically reformed the structure of education in the state so that the future will assuredly be better than the past.

There have been other results of great importance. The most

significant has been an unprecedented increase in state aid to local school districts, made possible by a limited sales tax. The commission's report has also inspired other states, notably Rhode Island and New Hampshire, to create similar statewide bodies to evaluate the public education system. The Massachusetts Advisory Council on Education, a unique body created by the commission's bill, has followed up, as it was meant to do, on a number of problems uncovered by the commission. It has now, for example, a statewide committee at work on plans to reform teacher education and certification, a committee that has at least the promise of doing work of significance in the state.

A national study of great potential has also grown out of the commission's work. One of the principal problems identified by the commission but not considered in detail was vocational education. Harrington and others on the commission found themselves extremely concerned at the end of the study about the quality of what passed for vocational training in the schools of the state; and about the failure of vocational education to reach great numbers of dropouts and students not going on to college. Harrington knew something had to be done but was not sure what. He took the commission's findings and his own concern to James R. Killian, Chairman of the Corporation of MIT and asked if MIT, with its unique experience in the Physical Science Study Committee and many subsequent curriculum reform projects, could do anything about the big unsolved problem of vocational education in American schools.

MIT did do something and is now conducting jointly with Harvard and Education Development Center (the New England regional laboratory that I discussed earlier) the first really comprehensive reform project in a field long neglected by the academic community. If this developmental study meets expectations, it could easily become the most important product of all, or rather by-product, of the Massachusetts commission. It could bring into the nation's schools an entirely new kind of *technical* education, quite unlike the old vocational education; and it could involve far larger numbers of students than any curriculum reform project so far.

Still another by-product of the commission is in the lessons it holds for other states. In my opinion, many of our states could profit immensely from appointing such a commission of their own and from studying the Massachusetts experience. That experience would indicate to them that the press can still move educational mountains. It would indicate the absolute importance of informed and vigorous leadership in the legislature, which Massachusetts luckily had in Kevin Harrington. It would indicate that the bitter-end battles likely to be put up by the establishment can be won with the help of uncowed politicians and an enlightened public opinion. And it would indicate that there are innumerable advantages for any state inherent simply in the creation of a reform-minded commission to look at the entire system of public education in the state.

We can see, then, in the work of these two extraordinary state commissions, the Massachusetts Special Commission and the California Citizens Advisory Commission, a means of influencing state education policy of great power. When such groups are broadly supported, they can have a major effect on the way in which the state governs its public education system. Both these groups, created by the legislature out of a sense of dissatisfaction with the educational status quo, were dominated by nonprofessionals and as such proved to be a powerful countervailing force to professional interest groups of the kind we have discussed in this chapter.

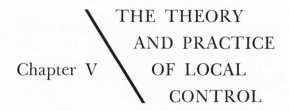

THE THEORY
AND PRACTICE
Chapter V   OF LOCAL
CONTROL

"HISTORY," said the English historian Froude, "is a child's box of letters with which we can spell any word we want." The same is true of what we Americans call "local control of education." We can use it to prove nearly anything. We can support social, political, or economic views of diverse and opposite kinds by citing the workings somewhere of local control of education; we can illustrate any virtue, any vice, and all virtues and all vices, with case histories of local school government. Again, it is the infinite variety of American education that makes it difficult for us to talk about one or another aspect of it as though it were a uniform quality.

Consider the diversity implicit in a few basic statistics about "local" schools. The United States Office of Education reported in 1966 that there were 31,705 local school districts in the country, and therefore 31,705 separate educational authorities (for the 1963–64 academic year; their number declines each year). The figures differ widely among the states. Nevada, for example, had only 17 of these school districts in 1966 for the whole state while next door California had 1,536. But population is not necessarily the controlling factor. Kansas in the same year had over 2,000 local school districts to serve its population of 2,237,-000 while Massachusetts had only 392 school districts to serve 5,361,000 people.

Minnesota and Tennessee have about the same population,

but the former governed its schools through no fewer than 2,148 local authorities in 1966 while the latter made do with 154. Vermont today has over twice as many school districts in relation to the number of school-age children in the state as does Arkansas. Illinois and Ohio have about the same number of children in the public schools, but the former has over twice as many local school districts as does the latter.

Current statistics indicate that, although the consolidation of school districts that has been going on for years continues at a steady pace, we are still one of the world's most diversified countries in the structure of our educational system. The NEA reports that there were 23,335 "basic administrative units" for public schools in 1966–67, of which 21,697 were "operating school districts." To oversee all these local units, which themselves represent a drastic reduction over previous years, there were 114,000 persons serving on school boards, but again not in proportion to population: Texas, for instance, had over 9,000 people on its school boards while Pennsylvania, with about the same population, had little more than half that number. Nebraska had over 8,000 board members while South Carolina had a total of 337. Well over half of all our school boards operate only elementary schools; a few operate only secondary schools; some operate no schools at all.

In addition to these thousands of local boards, nearly half of the states still have what the Office of Education calls "Intermediate Administrative Units"—that is, county school boards with or without county superintendents of schools. These boards cover two or more, usually many more, local school districts and thus stand midway between local boards and the state. While the county boards had an important role to play in the past (and indeed operated many schools of their own), they play a rapidly declining role now, except in the southern states where, outside the cities, the county board *is* the local school board. They still perform useful administrative and coordinative functions in states that have a great many small school districts, but even here are being eclipsed. Intermediate county boards and superintendents are rarely politically powerful any more, but they add to the administrative patchwork of American education.

About half of all our local boards have fewer than 300 students, some only a handful in a one-room school. But other districts, thought of as "local," have many thousands. Nearly two hundred American school boards have more than 25,000 students apiece under their jurisdiction. The New York City school board alone, with more than a million students in its schools, is responsible for the education of more students than are found in the majority of individual states. Los Angeles has as many students as the State of Indiana; Chicago as many as Wisconsin; Detroit as many as Mississippi. Or to look at it another way, nearly half of all the students in our public schools are under the control of less than 3 percent of our school boards.

What, then, we may ask, does "local control" mean? Can we seriously claim that "home rule" has the same strengths for, say, the Philadelphia school system with its nearly 300,000 students as for a school district in the Pennsylvania mountains that runs a single elementary school with 13 children? Should such boards have the same prerogatives and legal standing?

Such questions arise in other countries as well, though far less often than with us. Few countries of the world can match the nearly 90,000 units of local government reported by the Census Bureau to exist in the United States in 1962, which gave each county in the nation about thirty separate governments, many confined to governing schools. Such decentralization is extremely rare in the world. England and Wales, which except for Canada is the country closest to ours culturally and politically, has only 162 units of local government for the entire country and its nearly 50 million people, and these local governments act also as "local education authorities" to run the schools. Obviously, their school districts are much larger on the average than ours, but even so, local government in England will soon be consolidated into even fewer and larger units.

Variety in America is made greater still by the large numbers of private and church-related schools that operate side by side with our public institutions. Nearly 14 percent of all American school children are in nonpublic schools, the vast majority in Roman Catholic institutions. In many of our large cities, the nonpublic schools must be considered a second school system that directly affects the local government of public education. The local school system of Philadelphia, for example, where fully 40 percent of the students are in nonpublic schools, or New York City where 30 percent are, or Cleveland where 35 percent are, operate of necessity in an environment strongly conditioned by the fact that the nonpublic system saves the hard-pressed public system a great deal of money but at the same time tends to resist increased expenditures on the public schools. In cities such as New York where large numbers of independent schools (as distinct from Roman Catholic schools) operate, a great many students from middle and upper class homes are drawn off from the public schools, thus leaving these schools with a concentration of students who have special educational problems.

Oddly enough, the private school is now being promoted as one way of helping solve the educational crisis of the inner cities. Serious proposals are under consideration in New York City, Baltimore, Newark, and other cities, for contractual arrangements between the local school board (or between federal agencies) and private boarding or private day schools for the education of ghetto students. One of the most recent proposals, by a man experienced in inner-city education, is for "the creation of a national network of new, independent privately owned schools for the children of the nation's inner cities." [1] The adoption of any of these proposals would add greatly to the number of private schools, which might then begin to run the public schools a good deal of competition. It would be ironic, and possibly very salutary, if private schools were now to become a major influence on educational policy because of the inefficiency or incapacity of public schools.

The reorganization and consolidation of local school districts goes on steadily in America and in recent years has become a prominent part of the educational scene, as I will discuss presently. But diversity is still the main characteristic of local control and will be for some time to come.

School Boards and Their Evanescent Powers

The post of school board member is perhaps the most ill-defined in local government. The individual board member has no legal power, though the board itself is considered a corporation. The board's rights and responsibilities are rarely spelled out by the state except in the most general terms, and the board rarely undertakes to define them itself. The board's entire role and that of its individual members is simply an accretion of customs, attitudes, and extralegal precedents without much specificity. Many school board members and certainly many individual board members move in a sea of confusion about their powers. Some sail off in many directions at once, some drift with whatever winds are blowing from the school administration, some remain wholly becalmed and no doubt merit Mark Twain's quip that "First God practiced on idiots; then he made school boards."

In spite of my cautionary statements about the diversity of local boards and the difficulty of defining a "typical" board, I think it is possible to generalize in some ways. There is a kind of national pattern that is clear enough. The typical board will have five or seven members who are elected on a nonpartisan ballot; they will not have been "screened" by any quasiofficial body but will probably represent liberal or conservative political interests, broadly defined, in the community; the board will be made up mostly of men, about half of whom will have a college education and will therefore come from the professional and business groups; many members will have three or four years of experience on the board but one or two members will be new every year or so; members will be solid citizens but not particularly distinguished or powerful in their communities; the board will meet formally once a month (oftener now in many communities) in a public session and informally in two's and three's fre-

quently, though the board itself will avoid operating exten-
sively through formal committees.

And the board will shun politics like a plague, at least any
overt demonstration of interest in political matters. It will also
try to maintain the isolationist tradition of school boards. It will
strive, that is, to keep its special governmental status and will
insulate itself from the rest of local government, having nothing
to do, if possible, with the water, sewage, streets, welfare, or po-
lice departments. Thus the board will probably remain ignorant
of many things of which it should be aware, and will insure that
little if any coordinated planning between schools and the rest of
local government can take place.

But our model, which may serve well enough to represent the
numerical majority of boards, breaks down as soon as we look
at the big cities. New York, for example, has a nine-member
school board that is appointed by the mayor. By tradition, to say
nothing of political necessity, he sees to it that New York's big
three groups are equally represented: three Roman Catholics,
three Jews, and three Protestants. He also sees to it that the board
has at least one Negro or Puerto Rican. Chicago and other big
cities, and many small towns and suburbs, also depart sharply
from our model which, nonetheless, remains representative of
most boards.

The same argument that we saw with state boards about
elected versus appointed members goes on with regard to local
boards, and on the basis of as little evidence. One would be hard
put to try to prove the superiority of one method over the other.
But again the prevailing view among professional educators and
perhaps the public as well is, of course, that politics must be kept
out of education, and therefore that boards must be elected on
a nonpartisan basis. However, as should be abundantly clear by
now, politics and education are rightly inseparable, and politics
willy-nilly will play its part in tax-supported education, just as it
does in the educational systems of other democracies, particularly England where school board members are, *ipso facto,* mem-

bers of local partisan government. Whatever our own persuasion, we need not take the NEA seriously when it flatly classifies as "inferior" any method by which school board members are elected on partisan tickets and says that this conclusion is based on "the best professional judgment and practice," or on "the latest scientific evidence"! [2] But we can admire the audacity of the claim.

Our main concern is with the place of the local board in the political scheme of things and with the powers it is actually able to exercise. I believe that the powers of the local board, allowing always for variation, are greatly overestimated, and that American education does not enjoy anything like the degree of local control we like to think and are often told it does. If we look at any of the fundamental problems of education—defining the purposes of schools, establishing the curriculum, maintaining standards, getting good teachers and administrators—and at how much control over these critical matters is actually reposed in the hands of the local school board, we see that the board's freedom is in each case severely limited in three ways: its preoccupation with housekeeping details, its own failure to assert its authority, and the external controls forced on it by other bodies.

The local board's customary failure to distinguish between fundamental policy and housekeeping details is one of the abiding anomalies of local control of education. In theory school boards hire administrators to carry out the basic policies of the board and look after the details of running schools, but in practice more often than not the administrators establish the basic policies and the boards worry about the details. A number of case studies have been made of school boards in operation and all of them corroborate what ordinary observation would indicate: that school boards typically get bogged down in trivia and leave the most important decisions to somebody else, most often to the superintendent of schools. Typical of such studies is one by a professional educator who calculated that board members spend only 16 percent of their time on meaty matters like curriculum and standards, and the rest on managerial details.[3]

A more recent study took the form of interviews by the Gallup Poll with school board members across the country. One of the main findings was that,

> In most communities, school board members say they are overwhelmed by problems of immediate concern—finding enough money in the budget to meet school needs, trying to keep up with population growth with new buildings and classrooms, meeting the problems of teacher shortages, seeking able and experienced teachers within budget limitations. These tasks occupy most of the time of the nation's school boards. . . . In many communities the local school board does not devote much time to the discussion of the curriculum or to innovative practices, since these are left largely to the judgment of the superintendent, principals, and other members of the administrative staff.[4]

No doubt the reasons are many for this imbalance in the school board's activities, but one of the main ones, in my opinion, is that too many board members feel more comfortable dealing with specific administrative problems that have specific solutions than with philosophical or instructional problems that are much more important but are imprecise and difficult to grapple with. Like state boards, local school boards often lack staff as well to do research and background work for them, and to explore alternative solutions to problems; instead they must rely on professional educators, if on anybody, for such services. In any case, the fact is that the whole concept of local control of education is frequently undermined by the failure of the local board itself to exert the powers everybody says it has.

Controls from outside the school system are even more important in eroding the school board's power than its own failures. The state board of education and the state department of education are important sources of outside control, though they differ greatly, as we saw in Chapter IV, in the exercise of this power. Many states, such as Massachusetts, allow local boards to do just about anything not specifically *denied* by the state; others, such as California, allow local boards to do only those things specifically *permitted* by the state. But either way, the enforcement machinery of the state is usually so weak that a really determined board can go its own way. In other words, a school board *could* do much to neutralize the power of outside forces if it chose, but it usually does not so choose, and so in effect becomes the captive of other persons and groups.

New York State is distinctive in the authority of its State Education Department and is often criticized by local boards for abridging their freedom. A recent study by the New York Board of Regents found that the local boards within the state "did not in fact lead in the determination of policy, but act to implement and support programs determined either by the State or by professional administrators," and that fully 75 percent of the state's local board members felt that the state exerted either "far too much" or "somewhat too much" control over local boards.[5] Other states are less restrictive than New York but all do represent an important kind of external control limiting the autonomy of local boards.

More powerful still are what might be called the unofficial, and often unseen, controls exercised by outside bodies: by professional associations, accrediting agencies, institutions of higher education. Take the essential question of the curriculum, for example. Suppose a local board, aware of the obsolescence and flaccidity of much that passes for vocational training or "industrial arts" in the public schools, decides to reduce its programs in these areas. In theory this is one of its sovereign rights. In practice, several things occur to change its mind. First the vocational education lobby goes to work on other members of local government and on the state legislature or state department of education to protect the extensive interests of vocational education teachers. Second, the regional accrediting association comes to the aid of the status quo and makes threatening noises, suggesting and then perhaps demanding, on pain of disaccreditation for the schools involved, that the board rescind its decision. Third, the NEA state affiliate "investigates" and through its considerable power "persuades" the board to a different view. The point is not whether the board's decision is wise or unwise, but whether the board has the power, as we are always told it does, to control the curriculum. It does not.

We are told that one of the board's most important responsibilities is to hire the best teachers and administrators it can find. And indeed this is probably its most important duty. But in practice the board is free to hire only people who have been through what the professional establishment has decided is an adequate training program, but which, according to very widespread opinion among the public and teachers themselves, is frequently quite inadequate. If the board wants to hire, for instance, a person that the community may be fortunate enough to have in residence who has a record of intellectual or artistic or administrative achievement, but who has no education courses, it cannot do so. He may be an artist, writer, scientist, musician, or business executive of recognized standing and of a caliber that the board could not hope to match from the ranks of "trained" teachers or administrators; but the board is hamstrung not only by state certification laws but even more by the lopsided pedagogical course requirements of schools and departments of education in our institutions of higher education. (I discuss this problem in more detail and make a specific proposal for reform in the Appendix.)

So it is assuredly true that one of the greatest failures of local school boards is in their personnel policies, but that failure is fully shared by the professional establishment. School boards make one of their really critical decisions when they hire a new superintendent of schools, but anyone who has watched school boards set about the recruitment and evaluation of candidates would be under no illusion about how well boards carry out this responsibility. They often begin and end by asking the schools of education at leading universities to name some candidates, thereby yielding to these schools an influence that over time has come to be very great. Harvard's Graduate School of Education, for example, is said by many observers to exert through its Placement Office an important form of unseen control over education and to perpetuate its own kind of orthodoxy in the process. Teachers College (Columbia University) was for a great many years the nation's chief employment bureau for educational administrators and it is no fiction to say that the institution thereby exercised an important influence on the course of American education. On the West Coast, as one person thoroughly familiar with the situation remarked to me, "The University of Southern California's School of Education has operated a low-standard administrative mill for so long and churned out so many people that the majority of school superintendencies in Southern California are filled with their products."

In the equally important matter of hiring teachers, boards either turn over the recruitment and evaluation of prospects to administrators, thereby abdicating their responsibility, or they do their own evaluation but fail to set a firm standard. Many people believe, of course, that local boards *should* turn over the hiring of teachers to administrators and should avoid getting involved themselves; but most boards would acknowledge, I believe, that it is their clear responsibility to establish the standards for hiring teachers and to see that the standards are enforced. However, they fail to carry out that responsibility.

Few school systems even give examinations to prospective teachers. One would think examinations important at least for young teachers just coming out of training, in view of the exceedingly uneven quality of preparatory programs in the colleges and universities. Relatively few systems even give the National Teacher Examinations, a group of standardized, machine-scored tests administered by the Educational Testing Service (an agency that also administers the College Boards and a number of other standardized exams). For a variety of reasons having to do with the way in which "norms" are established for the National Teacher Examinations and the kinds of people ETS gets to write the questions, these tests are terribly weak, and it is just as well that they are not more widely used than they are. When I suggest the use of examinations for prospective teachers, I do not have these or any other established tests in mind, except perhaps for those now available in foreign languages; I have in mind the possibility of a local board's deciding that it must develop some better means than are now at its disposal for determining the abilities of prospective teachers.

One study in 1966 of large school systems found that only 12.8 percent of them "give examinations as part of the selection process and only 9.1 percent of the systems issue examination announcements for their vacant teaching positions." [6] The fault, however, is not wholly on the local level. After all, school boards are restricted in their search for talented teachers in the same way as they are for administrators: They are limited to hiring certain kinds of people who are said by agencies outside the local school district to be qualified.

How much real freedom do boards have in other basic matters? They must meet certain conditions to qualify for state aid. They must meet other conditions to get federal moneys. They must meet the curricular requirements of a variety of national testing agencies, not to mention those of individual colleges and universities. They may be restricted in the textbooks they can use or the kind of physical education they can offer. They may even be prevented by a teachers organization from instituting a merit salary scale.

Or suppose we look at what many people think of as the most important power of all of local boards, power of the purse. It is true that boards have control over school finances, but it is a control hedged about by many other forces. First, there are often state minimums that have to be met in such matters as teachers salaries, the largest item in the budget. Then there may be other state requirements relating to expenditures, and often other matters, that have to be met if the local system is to get its share of state aid. Then there are external agencies like the NEA whose statistics about comparative school expenditures can be used as a club to force the school board into larger budgets.

Then there is the fact that many school systems are fiscally "dependent." They must submit their budgets for approval to higher authority in local government, where they are frequently changed. They have no taxing power of their own. Even boards that are technically "independent," and they constitute a major-ity—boards, that is, empowered to approve their own budget and raise, directly or indirectly, the necessary taxes—are subject to strong pressures from other levels of local government, espe-cially the mayor's office. Since the checks and balances within the structure of state and local government are felt in much the same way by both dependent and independent school boards, the prac-tical difference between such boards is frequently small. In brief, power over the budget is undeniably one of the main controls still enjoyed by local boards, but even this freedom is a great deal less than complete and a great deal less than most of us think.

School District Reorganization and Its Political Effects

There is every prospect that the freedom of local boards will be reduced even further than has already been described as a result of the reorganization of school districts. Reorganization is a many-faceted movement of recent years that we need to pause to examine, for it has many ramifications so far as local boards are concerned. This movement is first of all a reflection of the steady urbanization of the country. Since the American Revolution when 95 percent of the population was rural, we have become a nation that is now 75 percent urban. But we have become more a nation of "metropolitan-area" dwellers than big-city dwellers. The main shift, that is, has been from the country to the city for the "disadvantaged" but even more from the small town and the city to the suburbs for the middle class. The Census Bureau now uses its "Standard Metropolitan Statistical Area" as a means of keeping track of these shifts. An SMSA covers any urban area of at least 50,000 people, and statisticians calculate that in an-other decade or so four out of every five Americans will live in one. There were 231 SMSA's in 1967 with an average of thirty-three school districts each, many of which were very small. The pressures for consolidation within these educationally fragmented SMSA's are going to be irresistible in the future.

A second factor in the movement to reorganize school districts is *de facto* segregation. The influx of Negroes and other minority groups into the central cities and the flight of middle class whites to the suburbs has now created a situation in which the majority of the country's nonwhites live in cities along with only a quarter or so of whites, many of whom send their children to private schools. This imbalance has brought demands for the abolition of existing school jurisdictions and the creation of new "metropolitan school districts" that would combine suburban areas with the central city. Although a few metropolitan areas have experimented with city-suburban programs, the authority for making such a radical reconstruction of school districts rests with the state legislatures. So far they have not shown much enthusiasm for the idea, but may find the accumulating pressures too great to resist in the future.

At the same time, however, there are demands to decentralize control over education within the existing big city systems—in effect, a counter-consolidation move. A 1967 study headed by A. Harry Passow (of Teachers College) of the District of Columbia school system, where Negro students make up 93 percent of the enrollment, recommended that the system be broken down into eight "subareas," each of which would have its own "community superintendent of schools" with genuine authority. Chicago announced in 1967 a decentralization plan that included a division of the city into three large school districts, each of which will be headed by an associate superintendent who will have a great deal of autonomy. Also in 1967, New York City, which has the largest and, so they say, the most rigid and ingrown school administration in the country, if not the world, announced a plan to give the thirty local school boards within the city, which had been purely advisory and quite ineffective bodies in the past, a great deal of additional power. They will have authority to make their own educational policies within limits, hire some of their own teachers and administrators, and in general run their own affairs.

A more radical solution to New York City's monumental school problems was proposed in November 1967 by a blue-ribbon committee appointed by the mayor earlier in the year and headed by McGeorge Bundy, president of the Ford Foundation. The Bundy Report strongly recommended a real decentralization of the city's school system that would divide the city into thirty to sixty school districts, each governed by a separate and largely autonomous school board. These parent-controlled boards would hire their own teachers and superintendents and would maintain only a tenuous link with a new central school administration. The present school administration reacted negatively to the Bundy proposal, which was recommended for adoption in 1969, fearing the capriciousness of local boards and the danger of their becoming tools of the most vociferous groups in the community. The New York AFT affiliate strongly objected on similar grounds. But some kind of decentralization, whether or not of the kind outlined in the Bundy Report, is going to take place in New York City in the near future and in other cities as well.

Such decentralization may be a more realistic expectation in the short term than the voluntary or forced merging of suburban and city systems, as has been recommended by various experts who say that the beauties of local control are mostly myths and the neighborhood school an outmoded way of organizing things. Certainly decentralization of big school systems and their massive bureaucracies in which the central administration is extremely remote from parents and teachers is more feasible politically than "metropolitanism." The civil rights movement is the chief impetus to metropolitanism, just as it is with big-city decentralization, but metropolitanism is a far more difficult and possibly dangerous change to bring about because it appears to many whites as a threat to the quality of their local schools as well as a death warrant for the kind of local schools that now prevail in suburbia.

In 1967 the Massachusetts legislature passed a bill that will create a new kind of school which is a sort of variation on metropolitanism. To be established is a state-supported public school, probably the first of its kind in the country, that will have its own school board and will mix students from inner Boston with students from the suburbs. It will operate, that is, on direct authority from the state and will not involve either decentralizing or recombining existing school districts. If successful, the school might well represent one way of resolving the political, financial, and social conflicts of metropolitanism; but the answer to any questions about its success are in the future.

In October 1967 a new journal called *Education News* announced the results of its nationwide survey on metropolitanism, and said:

> With the hesitant stealth of a reluctant dragon, metropolitanism moves across the nation. Its momentum is slow, its enemies many, its triumphs notable but few . . . [but] Without question, metropolitanism is the movement of the future. The only question is: How far in the future? [7]

How far in the future nobody can really predict, for there are no precedents to judge by. My guess is that we will see much more decentralization of city systems than creation of city-suburban systems in the immediate future. Either way, the politics of education in our cities are in for some rapid changes.

Still a third facet of the reorganization movement is the old problem of financial equalization. The disparity between the educational expenditures of the suburbs and the cities, and between the cities and the small towns and rural jurisdictions, is a complex calculation to make and one in which the many variables involved can never be given full justice. But there is no denying that the disparity is great, with some suburban school systems spending three or four times as much money per student as nonsuburban systems. Some cities have much more taxable property in relation to school-age population than the suburbs, but that often means that they get less money under the state's equalization formula while their children are much harder to educate and the demands on the city treasury for nonschool services much more extensive. Other cities have even less taxable property than their suburbs that have drained off not only the tax-paying middle-class families but much of the industry as well. So along with demands for metropolitan school districts are naturally coming demands for metropolitan taxing authority as a way of redistributing the money for education.

At the same time there are demands also for more money all around, regardless of what the structure of local school districts is to be. People claim that the main source of revenue for local schools, the property tax, is full of inequities (that it is regressive, does not reflect true property values, etc.), but even more important, that it is simply incapable of meeting school needs. People say that there is soon to be a taxpayers' revolt, although school revenues have increased by nearly 10 percent every year for the last decade, and two-thirds of all public school bond issues are regularly approved on the first vote.

In October 1967 *Education U.S.A.,* an NEA publication, announced the results of a survey it had conducted of school finances. It found that "17 states have boosted their support of public education more this year than in any other single year in their history. In addition, the gains achieved in 5 of the 17 states —California, Ohio, Maryland, Iowa, and Nebraska—are rated as massive advances." [8] One could make a fair case that local school authorities in the United States, whatever they say about the financial obstacles facing them, are raising more money for education, in either total or percentage figures, than ever before.

Tax experts themselves find it no easy matter to evaluate the property tax as the main means of school finance. "The American property tax," as one economist observes,

abounds in anomalies. During the past century, no major fiscal institution, here or abroad, has been criticized at such length and with such vigor; yet no major fiscal institution has changed so little in modern times. There is a vast literature on the property tax; yet less is known about its overall impact, incidence, and effects than is known about any other major tax. . . . There have been waves of criticism associated in time with the changing fortunes of the property tax: savage across-the-board attacks in the late nineteenth century; a somewhat more moderate tone and a quest for ways to make the institution work more effectively in the 1920's; renewed broadsides in the 1930's; and what can be best described as a "new complacency" regarding the property tax in the last decade . . . there is no such thing as "the" property tax. Instead, there are more than 82,000 local governments relying, often heavily, on a tax with a distinctive tax base and a distinctive tax rate. And while these 82,000 different taxes are set within a framework of fifty-one state (and District of Columbia) tax laws, the problem is further compounded by the enormous intrastate dispersion in both rates and tax bases within many states.[9]

Such dispersion is equally broad among the states themselves as well as among their local governments. The NEA's statistics indicate, for example, that per capita local tax revenues (chiefly the property tax) varied in 1964–65 from a low of $39.00 in South Carolina to a high of over five times that amount in New York. State aid, therefore, varies just as widely: In 1966–67 local school boards in Delaware got only 18.4 percent of their money from local taxes and well over three-quarters of their budgets from the state; on the other hand school boards in Nebraska and New Hampshire got nearly 85 percent of their funds from local taxes, leaving the state a very small bill. As a national average in 1966–67, public schools raised 52.1 percent of their money locally and 39.9 percent from the state, the rest coming from the federal government and other sources.

Whatever the arguments about the property tax, it is certainly true that many cities are now taxing at what they regard as the maximum possible rate, as indeed are many of the allegedly affluent suburbs whose educational growth in the last decade has far exceeded any growth in rated property values, and who are close to, if not at, their legal bonding limits. Thus arise inevitably the demands for shifting greater financial responsibility to the state, and then from the state to the federal government. Increased expenditures for any public function always, as one political scientist has commented, "tend to force a higher level of government to absorb a proportionate or increased share of the cost of that function; and this will be true in spite of habits and myths of local control and local responsibility. This proposition can be tested over the past generation in such fields as welfare, health, highways, and education." [10] James Bryant Conant in his re-study of the comprehensive high school put a major stress on the reform of school finance and endorsed the national trend toward greater state responsibility:

> In spite of the importance of education, proclaimed almost daily from the house tops (and political platforms), we have no deep and comprehensive study of the financing of public education state by state. There is not even a nationwide common practice, let alone a national policy. . . . As I have studied the problems of public secondary education during the last ten years, I have arrived at the conclusion that a radical overhaul of our thinking about financing public schools is required. My prejudices, I am frank to say, are inclining more and more to the belief that the financing of the public schools should be a state and not a local responsibility.[11]

If as seems probable the role of the states is to be increased in the matter of school finance, and certainly if finance is, as Conant recommends, to be a state rather than a local responsibility, there will be an accompanying loss of freedom by local school boards in the area where their freedom has been greatest. Local control will be further reduced through consolidation of school districts, though it may be possible for the larger districts thus created to resist state and national controls and outside pressures more effectively than small districts can.

The above discussion is not necessarily to say that school boards *should* have the kind of freedom that we customarily *think* they have, but which they in fact lack. How much control they should have as against that of the states or other bodies, and whether all boards should have the same control, are eminently arguable questions to which I will return. Our main concern so far in this chapter has been to look at how wide the gap is between theory and practice in the powers of local school boards.

The Power of Local School Administrators and Teachers

American schools are more lavishly administered than any in the world. The educational system of no other nation can come even close to matching the numbers of full-time, nonteaching school administrators that run our local school systems. The administrative hierarchy of some of our big city systems is larger than that of entire ministries of education in countries like England and France; even small town and suburban systems in the United States enjoy the services of many more administrators than comparable systems in any other nation of the world. This plethora of professional administrators, many of whom are more highly paid than state governors, university presidents, or our most distinguished scholars, is not an unmixed blessing. But it has a direct bearing on our central question: Who controls American education?

As I have already indicated, the balance of power in most local systems is strongly in favor of the superintendent of schools and of the administration generally, in large part because of the failures of the school board and of local teachers, both of whom, in my view, should exercise a greater voice in policy than they do. That the superintendent is a dominant force in policy decisions in many local systems is a proposition that would probably be resisted by administrators themselves, who like to say that the board makes policy and administrators carry it out, and by their professional association, the American Association of School Administrators, a 17,000-member department of the NEA. But it would be supported, I submit, by the overwhelming majority of experienced observers. It is also supported by most formal studies of local school politics, including those done by professional educators. Such studies are a relatively new specialty in education and reports that emerge from them are thick with the usual jargon and inflated scientism to which professional educators *cum* sociologists are addicted, but they are nonetheless worth our attention on the present question.

These investigators, many of whom can safely be assumed to be empathetic with school administrators and able to see their role in as favorable a light as possible, are nevertheless consistent in their criticism, as are political scientists and other people who have given the matter some kind of systematic study. I propose to let a variety of these investigators make the point in their own way so that my own view of the power of local school administrators does not seem merely a cross-grained private prejudice. Here, for example, is a typical judgment, based on the investigator's case studies of the educational systems of three contrasting communities:

> In the long run, the power structure of education revolves around the administration and the school board. These boards make up the vast majority of those who are concerned with educational matters on a sustained basis. Potentially the most influential are the administrators—especially the superintendent and his top aides. They are the ones who initiate action, who make proposals for change, who recommend that this or that be done. The school board and the community at large may accede wholly or in part to these proposals, or they may turn any of them down. But in the main the school board and the public pass upon the alternatives proposed by the administration. They rarely initiate proposals themselves. On a long-run basis, those who initiate the proposals will be the top figures in the educational power structure.[12]

Or consider these comments from a political scientist after a study of the incredible administrative jungle of New York City's educational system:

> One could accurately describe the situation in New York City over the past two decades as an abandonment of public education by key forces of potential power within the city. Max Weber's theory of the emergence of a specialized monopolizing power through its control of expertise describes the role of the education bureaucracy in New York City. The

claim that only the professionals can make competent judgments has been accepted by the public . . . it is the increased bureaucratization and overblown professionalization of the school system that has had the greatest impact on school policy making. The professional bureaucracy has manipulated its resources of expertise to discourage opposition and competing policies. The public's acceptance of technical expertise as the most relevant, if not the only, basis for sound judgment has furthered the depoliticalization of education policy. . . . It is almost certain that in larger cities curriculum, budgeting, and personnel policy are controlled completely by a headquarters bureaucracy.[13]

Another investigator made an extensive survey of "the literature" of professional education on the question of how much authority the superintendent of schools should have, and concluded that their claims to expert knowledge are not sustainable:

The literature clearly identifies democratic administration as the primary goal to be sought in administration of public school policy, but when the literature is analyzed in terms of democratic theory, it expresses a somewhat anti-democratic commitment to maximization of the superintendent's role in public school decision-making. These commitments are evident at every stage of a decision process. . . . Policy-making, described in the literature as the most important public responsibility in public school decision-making, is largely to be dominated by the superintendent's recommendations. . . . The literature also views policy application and appraisal as chiefly superintendent responsibilities. . . .

The literature fails to support the contention that the school superintendency is entitled to professional status and thereby to a predominant role in public school decision-making. Its discussion of administrative theory lacks a general theory of public school administration, and fails to demonstrate the existence of a body of knowledge distinctive to educational administration. . . .

The literature, in short, calls for extensive delegation of decision-making authority to superintendents, but does not really demonstrate why superintendents should possess such authority. It proposed decision-making processes for public education which raise serious questions for democratic government of the schools.[14]

Still another study of a similar kind arrives at this conclusion:

> Much of what was reported [in this study] cannot be condoned in the light of democratic values . . . the domination of a few leaders over school policies, as found in monopolistically controlled school districts, is not desirable, and educators should take no action which might tend to foster such tight power controls.[15]

A study reported by a group of professional educators in 1967, based on extensive interviews with school superintendents, emphasized the superintendent's pivotal role, for better or worse, in policy decisions:

> If the study of administration has resulted in any hard knowledge, it is the importance of the administrators to the maintenance of the organization, the pointing of directions for the organization, and the establishment of a climate that is either conducive to or frustrating of change and adaptation. As various studies have pointed out, the administrator is in a position either to promote broad participation in decision-making and creativity on the part of individuals in the organization or to run a tight ship and discourage the efforts of any of the participants to rock the boat. The administrator does more than set the climate for the participants of the organization. He establishes certain goals; he allocates resources; he develops the criteria for the selection of personnel; he is the bridge between the organization and the broader society from which he derives the resources with which it has to operate. He controls the use of sanctions, both positive and negative, within the organization, and by his use of them, he establishes the determinants for the behavior of subordinates. To the extent that the organization is adaptive, it is likely that there will be an administrator at its helm who provokes and encourages creativity and innovation within it. To the extent that the organization drifts aimlessly, it is likely to have an administrative head who is indifferent or

vacillating in his leadership role. To the extent that it is rigid and unadaptive, it is likely that there will be an administrator at its helm who restricts activity within relatively inflexible bounds.[16]

We could go on citing studies of this kind, such as one sponsored in 1965 by the New York Board of Regents in which a large number of school board members and superintendents in the state were asked, among many questions, this one: "In actual practice, whose views carry the greatest weight in the important decisions in each of these areas [such as the curriculum and the selection of staff]?" The responses indicated that the superintendent was allowed to make *all* such decisions.[17] But I am sure we have looked at enough comments to underscore my main proposition: that the superintendent of schools in most communities has accumulated an unconscionable degree of control over basic educational policy.

This adverse situation has come about for several reasons. It has come about, first, by default; by the local board's silence and its failure to carry out its responsibilities in the most important areas of the educational system, such as curriculum, academic standards, and personnel. If it yields its authority in these quintessential matters to the superintendent, it destroys its main *raison d'être*.

But the situation has also come about through conquest. In no other country, as I mentioned earlier, have school administrators managed to create the professional "image" they enjoy in the United States. In no other country could a professional association of school administrators follow an exclusionist policy of restricting membership, as does the AASA, to people who have been through what a voluntary professional association claims to be indispensable postgraduate training programs in school administration. But of course no other country has raised the whole field of "professional education" to the level that we have. The universities of no other country offer anything that even approaches the vast array of postgraduate degrees in educational specialties that is found in our institutions, and no other country has effected such a complete separation of school administrators from school teachers.

One may choose to believe that there does exist a large and esoteric body of advanced knowledge in how schools should be administered (a point I will return to in the next chapter), and that superintendents must acquire this knowledge in formal study at universities under theoreticians in schools of education; and that, having acquired it, they are justified in claiming the policy-making role they now have in local school systems. And indeed this seems to be at least the implied belief that prevails in many suburban communities—a seemingly strange situation that is explained by one political scientist this way:

> The technical expert, the district superintendent, is likely to flourish in those community settings where *expertise* and division of labor are assigned intrinsic value and where the citizenry is too preoccupied to attend to the matter of school government, or, for that matter, to municipal government. . . . Where his "employers" on the board and in the community trust and value *expertise,* he [the superintendent] is likely to have much more discretion and initiative, right up to the highest policy level.[18]

But I can only encourage anyone who seriously believes in this kind of educational expertise to take the trouble to look at, for a starter, the substance of postgraduate, especially doctoral, study in educational administration. He should see for himself the limits within which the study of school administration is commonly conducted. He will find in the great majority of our institutions that these degrees in administrative specialties, of which there are many varieties, are wholly under the control of the school of education and course work in them confined to that school's faculty. Such degrees have few academic prerequisites and are therefore taken with great frequency by teachers of physical education or of other nonacademic subjects, who then become school administrators.

Even professional educators are beginning to recognize that, if the local superintendent is to continue to dominate school policy, it would be better if he were himself a reasonably well educated person than if he were not. One of the studies I have already cited, based on extensive interviews with school superintendents, found them saying something of the same thing themselves:

> One of the major problems discussed by a number of superintendents was the level of competence of administrators. They claim there are too many incompetent administrators operating schools and holding membership in administrators' associations. . . . Little emphasis upon sociology, history, philosophy, political science and psychology is to be found in administrative training programs. . . . Numerous administrators became leaders by accident and not by design. . . . Much more attention also should be accorded to the recruitment process. Some superintendents feel that there are still too many jobs in administration filled with former coaches and bandmasters.[19]

A 1966 study of the school superintendency in New York State found that "more and more frequently [persons with] education majors, especially physical education, are being chosen [as superintendents]." It found that nearly a quarter of the superintendents appointed in the schools of New York State in the five years prior to the study had degrees in physical education. The study recommended that superintendents "have educational backgrounds rich in the liberal arts and sciences." It recommended that graduate schools of education "aggressively recruit students from disciplines in the liberal arts and sciences." It even recommended—and this is a radical step, even though the need for it has been clear a long time—that school boards sometimes consider hiring for superintendent someone who is not a professional educator but "an experienced leader who has demonstrated administrative and intellectual capacities in endeavors outside education." [20] As things are now, of course, nobody can be a superintendent of schools anywhere in the United States (with certain possible exceptions in New York and California), no matter how distinguished he may be intellectually or as an administrator of public institutions, who has not been through a stipulated training program in a school of education.

If neither the school board nor the community at large is able to put sufficient limits around the power of the superintendent, what about the teachers? One might assume that they are surely in a position to control many decisions and policies; certainly they are in some countries, such as England and Scotland, where the public school teacher has complete authority over matters of textbooks and instruction and where their headmasters think of themselves as teachers first, as *head* masters, and administrators second. The influence of teachers is also growing in the United States, mostly because there is so much room for it to grow, having been conspicuously absent in the past.

But the fact is that the American teacher has been dominated so long by administrators that his influence on policy continues to be exceedingly weak even in the face of the "new militancy" of the NEA and the AFT. This is so particularly in the cities, where the administrative structure is so large and pervasive, not to say intolerant, that teachers can rarely affect even matters in which their judgment is plainly superior to that of nonteaching administrators. A few years ago a study of the governmental structure of New Haven, Connecticut, came to a conclusion that seems to me equally applicable to the great majority of our cities:

> . . . for every nine teachers [in the New Haven schools] there is an administrator of some sort—a superintendent, assistant superintendent, supervisor, assistant supervisor, or principal. The school administrators rather than the teachers are the elite of the American public school system.[21]

Or consider the response to a massive survey conducted recently of teachers in California by a committee of the state senate. Over 16,000 teachers responded to questions on many matters relating to their work. Among the conclusions reached by the committee was the following:

> Attitudes of classroom teachers toward administration and supervision are of far more than academic interest.

American education is unique in the roles and relative influence on education assigned the two groups. In America the quaint tradition has developed whereby the nonteaching education personnel have become spokesmen for education in general. It is surprising that classroom teachers have with such docility surrendered their role as spokesmen even for what goes on in the classroom. Clearly, from the results of the two polls conducted by this committee, classroom teachers have entirely different priorities and values regarding education as contrasted with the values of the nonteaching educational spokesmen. It is shocking that these views seem to be óbtainable only under the shelter of anonymity as was provided by these questionnaires.[22]

As we saw in Chapter II, however, we are approaching a time when classroom teachers, because of the rapidly growing strength and determination of their professional organizations, will be able to exercise a greater degree of control than before. The NEA could have won such control for teachers in the past, had it not been so much a tool of school administrators. Now the mass of the NEA membership has been awakened by the fiercely competing AFT. Already the AFT chapter in New York City, the United Federation of Teachers, must be regarded as a major power in the making of educational policy, not only in salary matters but in other substantive questions about New York City schools. AFT groups in other large cities are rapidly following the New York lead and are thereby forcing local NEA groups in the same direction.

Collective bargaining for teachers, as I also mentioned earlier, is now assured by law in about a dozen states and will in all probability be so assured in many more in the future. Even where the right to bargain collectively with the school board is not embodied in law, it is being increasingly claimed by local teachers groups. In doing so they often put the superintendent into an ambiguous position. In collective bargaining he is presumably the agent of the school board acting in their interests, but he has been telling his teachers all these years that we need a "united" profession, by which he has meant membership in the NEA; as a fellow member of that body he must now represent the interests of teachers in bargaining. His position, in short, is untenable. It seems to me a safe prediction that the majority of American teachers will be covered by collective bargaining within a few more years. When they are, we may indeed begin to see a shift of power from the superintendent and other nonteaching local administrators to classroom teachers. But meanwhile, the school administration, not the local board and not the teachers, remains the primary locus of control over educational policy and over its implementation.

Parents and the Body Politic

I suppose the most persistent piety about local control of education in America is that it gives parents and the body politic a direct and active role in the management of their schools. Every textbook on school administration, every "Introduction to Education" course in our teacher-training programs, every pep talk by the local superintendent, every politician, theoretician, and pundit—each one stresses the importance of public involvement in the local schools. Parents should attend meetings, everybody says, do their homework on educational questions, speak up and make their views known, take a regular part in the life of the community's schools and, according to the establishment's gospel, *support* their schools.

But parents don't get directly involved, not 95 percent of them. Any more than they take an active part in local government generally or in the running of other community institutions. I have often been puzzled by the unflattering comments that educational administrators are apt to make in private about laymen and about how much of their own time and energies are squandered trying to reason with obtuse and meddlesome parents who don't understand either their own children or the purpose of the local schools. No doubt such parents exist, and no doubt some of them present their compliments to the superintendent from time to time; but I would hazard the guess that 95 out of every 100 parents with children in the public schools have never lodged a single complaint with the school administration or tried to make a single change in the local schools.

All is not apathy, however, for many parents would *like* to complain at one point or another in the course of their children's education, but the simple fact is that most of them are "nice" people who refrain from complaint for two reasons: they don't relish the possibility of a quarrel or other unpleasantness; and they are intimidated by the mystique of the administrator's expert knowledge. Parents may also appear apathetic because they believe that they can have little effect on school policy no matter how much they might complain.

An extensive study at Stanford University, based on interviews with parents about their attitudes toward their own schools, arrived at conclusions that merely reinforce what the ordinary layman's experience and common sense would tell him is the case. The investigators found that large numbers of parents felt that the polling booth "is the only voice voters have in schools." They also found that parents felt they lacked a grasp of educational problems. The report concluded that many voters

> have little sense of any efficacy in their relationship to the schools. They despair of their own ability to do anything, of the possibility that school officials might care about what they think, and they find educational policy too complicated for them.[23]

This is precisely the sort of situation that an organization like the PTA is, of course, supposed to prevent. But the PTA, as presumably everybody knows, is usually a creature of the local administration. It has been so assessed in many of the studies I have already cited, such as the case study of New Haven;[24] but studies are not needed to support such a proposition. I would merely appeal to common experience and observation, which seems to me a sort of massive corroboration of the obvious: that the American PTA is rarely anything more than a coffee-and-cookies organization based on vague good will and gullibility. It is chiefly useful to the administration for raising money for special projects and persuading parents who are interested enough to attend meetings that the local schools are in the front ranks of American education.

The problem with the PTA is leadership or the lack of it. The National Congress of Parents and Teachers has the largest membership, many millions of people, of any agency in education, though membership in itself does not mean much. The potential power of the PTA is therefore great. About half the parents with children in the public schools belong to one or another of the nearly fifty thousand local PTA's, where the membership is heavily skewed toward the elementary schools. There is an elaborate administrative structure. It begins with the national PTA offices in Evanston, where policies are formed that supposedly speak for the membership. The national office also tries to keep its members up to date by means of a flood of informative and inspirational publications. It has a legislative standing committee and also maintains a regular liaison with the major professional organizations in education. But I cannot remember any important issue on which the national PTA office has taken a position opposed to the NEA or the professional establishment.

Indeed the national PTA is a member in good standing of the "Big Six," a sort of behind-the-scenes association of three professional groups and three lay groups in education: The American Association of School Administrators (an NEA department that I have mentioned several times earlier), the National Education Association itself, the Council of Chief State School Officers, the National School Boards Association, the National Association of State School Boards, and the National Congress of Parents and Teachers. Some people might look on the Big Six as something of an establishment creature, as an instrument for promoting establishment policy rather than as what it is alleged to be: an instrument for hard-headed debate and bargaining among broadly based interests about what American educational policies should be. However that may be, the three lay groups on the Big Six, the national PTA in particular, are no match for the three professional groups.

There are state PTA's in all the states, but they rarely have any legislative or statewide influence; they seem to spend most of their time convening regional conferences. Then there are PTA districts within almost all states. Each district has a director who also spends his time in conferences and in providing general coordination and advice. Below the districts are the PTA councils, which are simply federations of the individual PTA's of the community. This elaborate apparatus may be required in view of the size and distribution of the membership, but it is cumbersome and helps to prevent the development of a strong national program or of a unified view on matters of consequence. In a word, the local PTA does indeed have an influence on educational policy: by failing to be more than an administrative rubber stamp, it simply sustains the existing order.

Only when an educational crisis erupts do American communities exhibit any significant degree of public discussion about educational problems, and even then the discussion is usually limited to a very small number of voters. In the great majority of communities the great majority of the time, the public's attitude toward education is simply apathy except as it relates to their own children's problems. In a detailed study of two contrasting communities and their "structures of power," one researcher put the number of citizens who played what he called "an active role in initiating and directing major community decisions," at .005 percent of the population,[25] a figure that would be acceptable enough, I believe, to other political scientists who have studied local government. The same can be said of other countries, incidentally, but other countries are much more centralized politically than we are, including England in spite of its 162 local education authorities.

Many superintendents of schools would hardly share this view. They talk a lot about the community pressures on them, by which they mean unwanted pressures for change, particularly from disgruntled parents. But when any large sample of superintendents is asked to be specific about these pressures in their own communities, they find the main problem is more often the layman's lethargy, or what they take to be his lethargy, than his involvement. One study of fully half the superintendents of schools of Massachusetts found very few of them conscious of much parental pressure; most of them put community lack of interest very high on their list of problems.[26] And in a study I cited earlier, school superintendents in New York State were asked to list and rate the community groups that had "some" or "considerable" influence on school policy. They listed a variety of business, church, farm, PTA, and fraternal groups, but indicated that none of them, with the single exception of taxpayers' groups, was opposed in any significant way to existing school policies.[27] In other words, what organizational influence there was on education in their communities was supportive of the superintendent and the administration.

But there are ways in which the public sometimes makes known its dissent from local school policy. Chief among them is the vote, which is exercised mostly on financial issues, where the body politic can indeed make its voice heard. The electorate, that is, can show its disapproval most easily by voting out a high-spending school board or voting down a bond issue. After studying forty-eight elementary school districts, one political scientist found, perhaps not surprisingly, that high voter turnouts bespeak dissent; but also that high levels of voting and dissent were characteristic of "districts low in aggregate indicators of social status, including family income, education and occupation. . . . Districts with low levels of dissent (and participation) were likely to be communities of high status. . . ." [28] In brief, the more affluent the community, the more willing it is to tax itself for education; and, as we saw earlier, the more willing it apparently is to believe in the expertise of the school administration—in part perhaps because affluent school districts pay their administrators high salaries and get the better ones. (It is also possible that lower-class districts in some states have high voter turnouts because of bought votes, hopes for patronage jobs, etc.)

But even in the most exclusive dormitory suburbs, the electorate will make its dissent known on occasion, especially when the board and the superintendent begin to take local support for granted. Again, the dissent is likely to be over expenditures and whether the community is getting its money's worth (an entirely worthy question). A recent study of voter revolt in one of the nation's leading school systems, New Trier Township High School District (outside Chicago), reinforces the point. Before New Trier's revolt, its school board and administration had grown accustomed to automatic support from their well-heeled constituency and had adopted a rather supercilious way of conducting school business. But the constituency handed the board a substantial defeat, the first one on record, in 1957 in the form of a vote of lack of confidence in the board's plans for school expansion. When the board did not respond adequately, the community handed it another stinging defeat in 1961. Finally the board and the administration began talking with, rather than at, the voters and got its amended plans approved. As one New Trier resident is recorded as saying, " 'The Board was of the opinion that if it *told* us enough times what it had decided to do, the community would buy it; for the first time, they're going to *ask* us.' " [29] Since 1961 the relations between the New Trier school board and its public, which in 1967 was putting up about $1,200 a year for each student in the schools (over twice the national average), have been exemplary.

But one must regretfully recognize that dissent in suburbia, or elsewhere for that matter, is very rarely over matters relating directly to the quality of education. Apart from recent outbreaks of parental disaffection in racially segregated schools, the layman rarely raises a question in public over standards or the curriculum, over whether social studies should be allowed to swallow up history and geography, over the quality of reading instruction, over whether girls should be compelled to take home economics or boys industrial arts, or over whether to establish a means of regular assessment of the district's schools.

When a local group of parents does decide to campaign about something important, their chances of success are not high. They sometimes get a hearing and sometimes are able to effect a few changes, but their batting average is exceedingly low. The local administration, often falling back on what "research proves," assures the unhappy parents that they are not abreast of "current professional thinking" and even suggests that they are no more qualified to comment than they are to tell the family doctor how to practice medicine. Or the administration can and frequently does use the regional accrediting association as a crutch or a threat, frightening the community with the possibility of dis-accreditation of the local schools if they fail to conform to professional ideas. The educational establishment, in short, has most of the weapons in such encounters with laymen.

Even with academicians, the establishment can usually mount an effective counterattack. Consider, for example, the case of the San Francisco Curriculum Survey Committee. In the summer of 1959 the San Francisco school board, aware of the dissatisfaction of a great many people with American education in general and with California education in particular, appointed a committee of outstanding subject matter scholars from Stanford and Berkeley to survey the quality of academic study in the city's schools. The board's assumption, quite rare among school boards, was that such persons were eminently qualified to evaluate textbooks and teaching methods in their own subjects. The board deliberately declined to put any professional educators or administrators on the committee.

Nine months later, in April 1960, the committee handed a highly critical but constructive report to the school board. It found much to quarrel with in the materials and methods used in the teaching of academic subjects in the city's schools and made cogent recommendations for reform. The superintendent of schools in San Francisco, a solid establishment figure, produced a reply to the report in May in which he guardedly admitted the validity of some of the criticisms, especially those that had already been aired in the city press, but subtly questioned the competence of the investigators. By June the establishment had organized its forces sufficiently to get out a strident manifesto signed by seven professors of education from San Francisco State College in which they impugned the motives and the talents of the scholars and their report. This document was followed by still another one signed by eight liberal arts professors from the same institution in which they attacked the attackers.

The point is that when all the smoke cleared away, the San Francisco schools went on just as they had before. Nothing changed. And that is the customary fate of local committees and groups that try to push school reforms against the opposition of the local administration. One could fill a small library with the histories of such groups. Some good is no doubt done simply through a local airing of the educational issues, whether or not changes are made; at least the public discussion may contribute to creating a climate of opinion in which reform is made easier in the future. But the fact remains that the only educational pressure groups that are regularly successful in local school districts, and even they are small in number, are those aimed at raising more money for education or that promote other causes favored by the school administration.

I do not mean to suggest that any pressure group that comes along with its pet reforms deserves to succeed. We all know that political fringe groups, for example, can make life extremely difficult at times for teachers and administrators. When they do, a firm school board is the best insurance against unreasonable demands. If the board is not firm, such groups often succeed. But it is easy to overestimate their number and their importance, for they are usually newsworthy and their activities get a lot of press coverage. But in fact such incidents are few in relation to the number of school districts. If the NEA's sleuths, who now keep secret dossiers on any person or group that criticizes American schools, were to make public its files over the last ten or twenty years, I would guess that we would all be surprised by the relative scarcity of local incidents wherein political or other fringe groups have made any effective changes in the schools of the community. Of course special nonpolitical interests can occasionally capitalize on a receptive or an apathetic public to effect a major change in schools. Driver training, for example, is now a standard item in American schools because the automobile and insurance industries were able to create or bring out sufficient support for it from legislators, school administrators, and the public.

The future, as we have so often noted in this book, may be dif-

ferent from the past. The ramifications of the civil rights movement and of the numerous poverty programs are great in education. Already we find violent and unprecedented attacks on the
entrenched professional hierarchy of big city school systems, and
we find uncompromising demands being made—and met—for a
parental voice in educational decisions, including the hiring of
teachers and administrators. In 1966 a self-styled "People's School
Board" in New York City brought suit in the courts to prevent
adoption of the regular school budget, complaining that the
city's regular school board had "yielded its policy-making authority to the school system's professional staff." The People's School
Board was not successful but it helped to prepare the ground
for the recent expansion of powers for local district school boards
that I mentioned earlier, in which parents are supposed to play
the role we have often been told they should play in American
education. This kind of change—and one can easily look with
fear, even horror, on it—may well be the wave of the future in
the cities and may ultimately wash over the suburbs and small
towns as well, though with a different motivation on the part of
parents. Even those who sympathize with the change may be dis-
appointed for a while at the dogmatism or sheer inability of laymen and the body politic in the making of school policies in the
inner cities, but the shift of power from professionals to parents
may at worst be no worse than what the cities have had up to now
and may well be better after a period of apprenticeship.

Still, the most fitting thought with which to close this discussion of local control of education is that parents and the body
politic are normally effective in American education only when
they support the local school administration. This would be cause
for rejoicing if one were satisfied with the educational status quo.
But if the status quo needs changing, we can only regret the
lack of influence on the part of that entity that is supposed to
give local control of education its meaning in America—the
electorate.

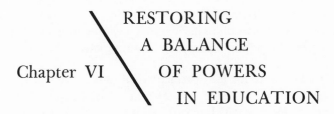

Chapter VI

RESTORING
A BALANCE
OF POWERS
IN EDUCATION

THE READER by now is abundantly aware that the question with which we began—who controls American education?—hardly lends itself to a plain and simple answer. Nor does the concomitant question: "Who *should* control American education?" But I believe we have answered the first question well enough in the foregoing chapters to enable us to answer the second. We have seen that the important decisions in education emerge from a labyrinthine structure of forces and countervailing forces, but that the interests of professional educators tend to be dominant. We have seen that other interests can have a strong and even controlling influence—as demonstrated, for instance, in the power that public opinion exerted after Sputnik on behalf of educational reform—but only on rare occasions. And we have seen that at least the beginnings of change are now evident in the militancy of teachers, the demands of Negroes in the inner cities, and in the work of the curriculum reform groups. We have, that is, described the complicated political pattern by which American education is presently governed.

Having done so, we need to consider one or two of the fundamental ways in which the pattern might be reconstructed. Of necessity these ways, like the problem itself, lack the precision that naturally appeals to reformers. It would be comforting to think we could solve our problems in the politics of education through some series of numerable, specific acts—for example, elect all members of state and local school boards on nonpartisan, or partisan, tickets; appoint them all by the mayor or the governor or the legislature; decentralize city school systems into districts of five thousand or fifteen thousand students; restrict administrators to housekeeping chores; abolish schools of education.

We must, alas, settle for less spectacular solutions that will repair but not revolutionize the government of education; that will foment no insurrections but will perhaps restore something approaching a balance of powers in what is now an imbalanced situation. I have frequently touched in the previous chapters on the kinds of remedies needed, but in this final chapter I would like, at the risk of repetition, to bring my thoughts together under two broad headings, one having to do with the relations between experts and the body politic, and the other looking once again at the relations between the federal government and state and local authority.

Experts and the Rest of Us

By "experts" I mean those people who call themselves, and whom we have called in this book, "professional educators." And by "the rest of us" I mean exactly that: everybody else, laymen, politicians, academicians, students, and classroom teachers. This polarization may seem oversimple, especially since I would like to see the term "expert" expanded beyond its present applications, but I think it serviceable enough in illuminating the imbalance with which we are concerned. After all it is, as we have seen, the experts—the school administrator, the professor of education, the accrediting officer, the staff members of state departments of education, and the managers of numerous professional organizations—it is these experts, sharing much the same background and outlook and having been through homogeneous training programs for advanced degrees in schools of education, who lay claim to special knowledge that is supposed to distinguish them from "the rest of us." It has been out of deference to this specialized knowledge that the rest of us have allowed the expert to exert as much control as he now does over educational policy.

If I could leave the reader with only one impression in this book, I would like him to take away the conviction that all of us have badly overestimated the quality and the extent of expert knowledge in education. As a consequence there are rather too many experts in our educational system of the kind described recently by Harold Howe, II, United States Commissioner of Education, in speaking about his fellow professionals:

> . . . no matter how erratic and unproductive a lay-directed policy system in education may occasionally be, I think we must recognize that specialization brings its own dangers. Professionals in any field sometimes purchase their depth of knowledge at the expense of breadth. The professional, left unchecked, is liable to become a dictator; a school superintendent is no more exempt from becoming a hometown Hitler than the most pompous and arrogant Babbitt who ever headed a school board. . . . The roots of the word [layman] itself are instructive: it was first used to distinguish ordained ministers and priests of a religious congregation from the rest of the flock. I suspect we educators sometimes tend to regard ourselves as anointed by a holy oil that confers a unique wisdom upon us, and that we literally regard laymen as a flock: sheep to be herded toward a destination we have picked out.[1]

Thus the dictum propounded to the dismay of many professional educators by Francis Keppel when he preceded Howe as Commissioner that "education is too important to be left to the educators" deserves to be taken seriously by laymen, not merely because education is indeed important but because the judgments of nonexperts are frequently as valid in education as those of experts.

Laymen badly need to sensitize themselves to the limitations of educational expertise; they need to realize how quickly the limits of knowledge are reached in regard to any fundamental question that can be asked about education. Whether it is a question of educational aims or philosophy, of what subjects should be studied and for how long, of whether and how schools or teaching should be evaluated, of whether and how students should be divided by ability, of testing intelligence and what intelligence means, of "compensatory" education, or of any other substantive matters that can be named, the expert's knowledge is not good enough for the rest of us to leave the policy decisions to him, not nearly good enough.

Nor is it much better with respect to the role many laymen think the expert *should* play: that of telling those who are supposed to make decisions what will happen if they make this or that decision from the range of choices that may be open to them on any given problem. Rarely can the expert, whatever he may say or believe himself, speak with real authority on the consequences of one educational action or another. Educational prognosis is on a par at best with economic predictions or weather forecasting or stock market analysis. Educational experts are better at explaining the past than predicting the future, though they will be right a certain percentage of the time.

The reasons for the expert's inexpertness in education are surely not far to seek. Professional education as a subject of formal study is still new, though older than many scientific and technical specialties that do indeed produce concrete results of fundamental importance and do have great predictive reliability. But nobody yet knows what the "field" of professional education is. It draws on many other fields, but has not yet developed experimental methods or analytical instruments of its own with which to advance knowledge or make reliable recommendations.

One has only to look at what passes for educational research on any of education's most significant problems, and this can be a painful experience, to realize how uncertain must be a decision based on such research. Take, just as one example among many possibilities, the whole controversy that has swirled around the teaching of reading to young children since the publication in 1955 of Rudolf Flesch's book, *Why Johnny Can't Read* This protracted quarrel, which I referred to several times earlier, has produced a genuine polarization between the bulk of the experts and the bulk of parents, the latter claiming vehemently that "look-and-say" doesn't work and that "phonics" does, and the former claiming vehemently that parents are wrong because "research proves" the efficacy of look-and-say. The look-and-say method of teaching reading, thanks to the proselytizing efforts of the experts, many of whom have a substantial financial stake in look-and-say textbooks, has monopolized reading instruction in American public schools for many years.

Reading experts accomplished this coup because of the lack of dissent or at least of any visible minority opinion within their own ranks. The conquest of American schools by look-and-say is an illustration of what one political scientist suggests as a general rule: "As long as there is substantial agreement among educators, the claim to detached, professional expertise is plausible. If there is disagreement among 'the experts,' however, the [school] board or the public must makes its choice among alternatives. . . . Lay or public control is enhanced by division among educators." [2]

Fortunately large numbers of laymen, critics, and such groups as the Council for Basic Education and the Reading Reform Foundation have chipped away so relentlessly at the solid front put up by the orthodox reading experts that some reconsideration of the schools' commitment to look-and-say is now occurring. And the country is at last getting a variety of good phonics systems and textbooks.

"Research" in reading, however, has been strongly on the side of the experts, since it was conducted by them. There has been a mountain of it over the last quarter of a century. But parents have wisely suspected that this research was something less than compelling and might not "prove" anything. Their suspicions were finally confirmed in 1967 when for the first time a really comprehensive study of this body of research was made, even though it was made by still another reading expert. The investigator's report, while couched in the most charitable terms allowed by the findings, is nothing less than an indictment of the quality of this research and of the missionary zeal of those who have sold it to the teacher-training institutions and to the public schools.[3] (One might well ask, of course, why we should accept *this* research on reading research. Perhaps we shouldn't, but it would be more than human for the advocates of phonics not to accept new research that underscored how bad the old research was.) The same conclusion, I am confident, awaits many other areas of educational research; reading research is merely one subject among many from which experts derive their expertise.

What, then, should a layman or a school board do to get expert advice as a help in making policy decisions?—for I am not suggesting that such advice is without merit or that professional educators, especially when they speak from practical experience and not research, cannot advise and consent with a measure of authority on many questions. First, the layman can simply cultivate a sturdy skepticism as to how much is really known, by experts or anyone else, about the important problems of education. He should get used to the idea that many more decisions must in the end be made in education on the basis of faith, hope, and common sense than on hard evidence. He should listen to the experts, by all means, and get whatever facts are available, but he might remember that, as John W. Gardner puts it, "If a modern leader doesn't know the facts he is in grave trouble, but rarely do the facts provide unqualified guidance." [4]

He should make a point in particular of listening to more than one expert. He should beware of anyone whose advice is based principally on research claims or peremptorily on "the best current professional thinking." In a word, he must seek expert advice but must learn to evaluate it; and, until a lot more is known about education than is now known, he must regard with great skepticism the solutions to educational problems that may be offered to him with great certitude by experts.

Second, the layman can try to keep the line between the responsibilities of citizens and experts reasonably clear. It is constantly being clouded by both groups, in part because there really is a twilight zone between their roles. The layman is often found telling the professionals how to carry out policies while the professionals are even more frequently found telling the layman what the policies should be. Experts are forever telling us, for example, that education should be expanded: They tell us we should have many more community colleges, or that higher education is a right in our society and not a privilege.

Or we find experts at the Educational Testing Service telling us, not how tests might help us achieve whatever educational goals we as a society set, but who should be admitted to college and how we as a nation ought to be setting about the business of higher education. Experts are forever telling us what the aims of education in our society should be, not how to achieve the aims that society itself might establish. They tell us, not how social studies should be taught if social studies is what we want, but they tell us we should want it. They tell us, not how compensatory education should be carried out, but that American society should support it. Not infrequently they tell us that schools should seek to build a new social order and that they, the experts, know what the new order should be.

On all questions about what we Americans want or should want in education, the expert's opinion may be worth our attention but we should never allow the expert to make the decision. When the expert claims to speak with some kind of special wisdom on such questions, we might listen respectfully but guardedly, preserving our determination to assess, not merely accept, what he tells us.

No doubt many educational experts, and perhaps some intellectuals, would disagree, arguing that an educated man has achieved a general intellectual competence that gives his views more weight, both in the area of his specialty and on public questions, than the views of men with more limited education. Perhaps. But I doubt that the level of education or intellectual acumen of most educational experts is all that much higher than that of laymen who are usually found in policy-making positions in education. Moreover it is not at all clear that many of the fundamental decisions to be made in education are better made by people with postgraduate degrees than by people with merely undergraduate degrees or no degrees.

A third step that laymen can take to get expert advice in education is to expand their conception of who is an expert. On many questions with which school boards and other citizens groups must deal, professional educators represent only one kind of expertise. Laymen should, in my opinion, invite the views of other sorts of educational experts. They might, for example, solicit the advice of teachers themselves far more often than they do, particularly on matters of curriculum, discipline, textbooks, and problems of school operation. Teachers commonly sit as "co-opted" members of educational policy-making boards in other countries, but have been squeezed out of such positions in America.

The last White House Conference on Education brought together over seven hundred "experts" and laymen to talk about educational policy in the nation as a whole, but there were scarcely a dozen classroom teachers in the entire congregation of delegates. Significantly the almost total absence of teachers did not strike most of the experts in attendance as remarkable, any more than did the scarcity of school board members.

Nor does it apparently strike most professional educators as somewhat grotesque that the newly formed National Academy of Education gives so little recognition to *teaching* as an activity at least as important as any other in education. The NAE was supposed to be a sort of National Academy of Sciences for education, a prestige association to which were to be invited to membership the nation's leading educators. But unlike the science academy whose members are chosen because of their stature as practitioners—as working scientists—the education academy set up four categories of members not one of which is for eminence in the practice of education, that is, teaching. The same failure to listen to teachers or to respect *their* expertise has long been evident in national educational organizations, in accrediting agencies, in state education departments, and in the deliberations of local school boards.

In Chapter II we examined the surprising pugnacity that teachers are exhibiting these days and the prospect that their professional organizations will soon become a major force in the making of educational policy—speaking, that is, for teachers. Some of us who have long lamented the timidity of teachers in the political arena of education and strongly urged them to assert themselves may not be entirely comfortable with the direction their "new militancy" is taking. The prospect of a massive and monolithic national teachers organization bent only on extracting as much money from school boards as possible, under threat of a strike, is not salutary. But the belligerence is understandable in view of the past and may well be lessened in the future by giving teachers a greater voice in running schools than administrators and school boards have been willing to give them up to now. In any case, laymen would be well advised to expand their conception of who is an expert in education to include the teacher.

The layman could also lend an ear to college teachers and to academic scholars who offer a different kind of expertise from that of the professional educator. Certainly on matters of course content, textbooks, the "new curricula," on the qualifications and training of teachers, and on many other subjects, the academician who also has some knowledge of the public schools could be of excellent service to a local or state board of education and to other bodies charged with policy responsibilities. But the scholar is rarely consulted now by such groups.

Fortunately the curriculum reform movement of the last decade has been the means of restoring the scholar to an important role in school affairs. There is even talk now about the coming of a "new establishment," in which the academician plays a central role, displacing the old. Many observers believe they see a new educational establishment being formed by scholars, critics, civil rights leaders, foundation officials, and perhaps the federal government through people like John W. Gardner and Harold Howe, II. James Bryant Conant echoed this theme when he commented that the

era of nationwide school policy planning by unofficial agencies reflecting only the opinions of the establishment is drawing to a close. As an interstate planning agency for the public schools, the network of NEA-affiliated state organizations is coming to be less and less effective; as a method of enforcement, the regional accrediting agencies are rapidly losing ground.[5]

I wish I could share this view, and I do to some extent. But the staying power of the *ancien régime* also impresses me, and I don't see the old guard withering away or being put to flight for some time. Rather, I see a kind of prolonged coexistence, sometimes peaceful, sometimes combative, at the end of which we may indeed have a new establishment which will be a great improvement over the old, but which may also develop its own problems.

Consider the present state of any of the big controversies that have characterized American education in the last fifteen or twenty years. The long fight over progressive, modern, life-adjustment education is considered won by many people who feel that the establishment has been put to ideological rout. But I regret to say they are mistaken. Progressive education is far from dead and chances are that you have only to look as far as your neighborhood school to see how alive it still is. We have had, that is, some success in reducing the size of the curricular smorgasbord for the brighter students and possibly in reducing the more frivolous ways in which many average and below average students used to spend their time in school; but we are a long way from either forcing or persuading the establishment to give all students a sound basic education.

We have made progress in teacher training, one of the most important and inflammatory of our problems. But anyone who thinks there is a new establishment in charge of the vast industry of training and licensing teachers and administrators in this country has his head in the sand. State certification laws are pretty much the same as they ever were; institutional course requirements are a bit better but are still far short of a major reform; students coming into training are better in some institutions, the same in many, worse in some; accreditation of teacher-training programs is still done by the establishment-dominated National Council for Accreditation of Teacher Education; and school boards have very little more freedom than they ever had in the kind of people they can hire. The establishment is even mounting a counterattack, as we saw earlier, in those states, such as California, where there has been some genuine progress in licensing practices. So again, the new establishment, if there is one, has had very limited success in displacing the old.

In the same way one could go down the list of our major educational problems and what has been done about them, but the point would remain the same. The professional establishment, though somewhat diminished, is still extremely powerful. It has lost some of its control to a new breed of educator and to new and happier coalition of "outside" interests, but it is far from eclipsed and will continue for some time to enjoy too large a voice in educational policy.

The layman's best defense, then, against both old and new establishments is a determination not only to assert the principle of lay control of educational policy but to make it a fact. His best insurance against the expert is a keen awareness of the limits of educational expertise. His best defense against his own limitations is to make a habit of listening, not only to a variety of professional educators, but to a variety of teachers and other kinds of educational experts.

His best tactic when challenged by the professional educator to do more than complain, to come up with what the professional likes to call "constructive criticism," is to have some concrete proposals to offer that he feels will fit particular problems in his own community or broader proposals that have been made by others and that he supports. One of the best ways for him to learn about specific reforms, programs, and practices that might be adopted by, or adapted to, his community is to read the monthly *Bulletin* of the Council for Basic Education (725 Fifteenth St., N.W., Washington, D.C. 20005). As I mentioned in Chapter III, I have been associated for many years with this organization and am not embarrassed to commend it in this fashion since it is the only organization that offers laymen the kind of specific ideas he needs about educational reform.

As a further example of a specific program of action, one that in my opinion is applicable to every state in the union, I have reprinted in the Appendix a proposal that I made early in 1968 to the Massachusetts Advisory Council on Education. It is a proposal for reconstruction in one of the most important parts of our educational system, the training and licensing of teachers and school administrators. The heart of my proposal is the creation of a new mechanism to govern teacher education and certification that would represent the kind of balance of powers that we have been talking about here. I don't offer it necessarily as an ideal solution, but it is at least a concrete proposal that seems to me to have application not only to the other states but to other areas of the educational system as well.

In a word, the layman can only recover his proper role in educational policy by taking it. The English have a saying to the effect that the expert in any field is to be kept on tap by those who make policy, but not on top. It is good advice for the American layman, but I am not sure that he will act on it.

Creative Federalism and All That

There are no easy or obvious answers to the conflicts created by the new "partnership" that the federal government has assumed with the states and cities. The federal determination to take on problems that lower levels of government fail to tackle is continually running afoul of state and local authority in education. But for most people the main conflict is no longer ideological, no longer a fight about whether the federal government *should* help to solve particular educational problems. The main conflict is only over *how*. Of course there are still many people who feel the federal government has no business whatever in education, not even to the extent of sharing taxes with the states, and they can make a case for their position; but they are swimming against a swiftly moving mainstream. "The States' Rights position," as one economist observes,

> whatever its logic and more content, has historically become progressively less of a guide in determining the direction of public policy as American history has run its course. The more vexatious problems of the nation have, for better or worse, been viewed as national and have ultimately called forth congressional and federal administrative action. A few examples will suffice to indicate this: the restriction of child labor, minimum wage, social security, pure food and drug statutes, holding company legislation, the military draft, and agricultural policy. These and other legislative and non-legislative issues have come within the permanent concern of the federal government. This is not to argue that such concern is necessarily justified by ultimate philosophical and moral values. The flow of history simply reveals that concern with knotty matters which have their incidence on local communities, states, or, more importantly, on individuals, have often been the subject of federal assistance and legislation with public approval.[6]

But the urgency of special problems such as the education of deprived children is not the only reason for the growth of federal involvement in education. The general redistribution and equalization of educational expenditures is an even stronger impetus to federal action. The drive is for equalization not only among the fifty states but among the school districts within them as well. The 1965 Education Act was an effort to deal both with special problems and to some extent with the problem of unequal resources in general. It seems clear that the 1965 Act is merely a prelude to a greatly expanded federal participation in the future, particularly if, as seems likely, equalization is not pursued more vigorously than is now the case at the state and local level. Either way, the taxes will have to come, as two political scientists point out, from the same segment of the population:

> Whatever means are used to provide the resources for the provision of adequate education services, they will have to

come, in large part, from the middle- and upper-income suburbanites. If, therefore, the suburbanites resist a redistribution of population or a redrawing of school district lines to
create a more equitable balance in the present pupil ability
distribution, the alternative—if the problem is to be met—
is greater Federal and state taxes paid by persons of middle
and high income.

The fundamental issue, therefore, really revolves around
the ability and willingness of Federal and state governments
to raise revenues and redistribute the resources according to
need.[7]

In other words, there will be a marked redistribution of taxes
for education, one way or another, in the immediate future, even
as there now is on a limited basis. Since state and local government will probably not take the lead in such a redistribution, the
federal government will. Again I refrain from comment on the
political wisdom or unwisdom of this movement; our concern is
with its effects on educational policy.

Virtually everyone agrees that federal money for education is
better channeled through the states than handed out directly
from Washington to individual school systems, *provided* the states
are equipped to handle it well. Surprisingly, there seems to be a
liberal-conservative consensus in the making about the importance of retaining state authority in education. From the most
improbable sources one hears references these days to "the federal octopus" or to "the Washington pork barrel." Numerous
professional educators seem to have discovered that federal funds
available for education are often incredibly mismanaged by the
Washington bureaucracy. And so educator and politician alike
now call for some kind of revenue sharing or for general, un-
categorical aid from the federal government to the states. This
is one of the major aims of the National Governors' Conference,
which in 1967 opened an office in Washington to promote the
interest of the states (it used to be called states' rights) against
the federal monolith. And of course the PTA's, the school boards
association, the state superintendents of education, and other

groups whose natural bias is toward local and state control of education are pretty solidly on the same side.

The only problem seems to be the continuing inability of the states to handle federal funds wisely or to distribute them equitably. Because of this incompetence, the states have been bypassed in a number of federal education programs (just as they have been in other areas, such as labor relations, transportation, and welfare), at the same time that their fiscal responsibilities have been growing at a far greater rate than those of the federal government; their expenditures, as one economist calculates it, have grown at least 20 percent faster than the Gross National Product, while their taxes have barely kept pace with the GNP.[8]

Even so, the consensus in education seems to be that the states should reform and should develop an adequate capacity to act as intermediaries between the federal government and the local school districts. But it is not a strong consensus, for there is a widespread fear in and out of education that the states will remain quite incapable of handling federal funds well as far into the future as can now be seen. Some people would cite the misuses or unfruitful uses to which the states have already put Title V federal funds as clear evidence of the dangers of relying on state reform. Others would point out that state legislatures could not do anything with general federal aid except distribute it evenly across the state, which would defeat the whole idea of the federal government's yielding control to agencies closer to the grass roots in order to solve problems on a priority basis.

In any case the states may well be able to recover in the near future a good deal of their lost control over education, for better or for worse. John W. Gardner was probably reflecting a general feeling in the education community when he asked a Senate committee in 1966 to "consider the future relationship of the Federal Government to State and local government," and went on to say that

One possibility that one could easily imagine is that increasingly large sums of money flowing to weak State and local governments might eventually bring about complete subordination of the latter. All State and local governments would then be mere branch offices of one all-dominating National Government. I can't believe that any sensible citizen relishes that possibility. . . . A second possibility is that the federal government—impatient with the inadequacies of many State and local governments might begin to create its own network of local instrumentalities. If the local schools and social agencies aren't doing an adequate job with disadvantaged youth, the Federal Government is tempted to create separate Federally-financed programs or agencies to do the job directly. This approach is observable in a number of current programs. . . . A third possibility is the one to which President Johnson has given his blessing. We can proceed down the path of a Creative Federalism that puts the Federal Government into a healthy partnership with State and local governments. President Johnson conceives of this partnership as one in which the integrity and autonomy of State and local government is jealously guarded by all concerned.

This is a noble conception, but involves one stern requirement—strength and vitality at the non-Federal end of the partnership. It will not be possible to fashion a mutually respecting partnership if State and local government is not able to play its role as a vital partner. So we shall have to consider the question of strengthening State and local government.[9]

Whether the states will be able to strengthen their administrative and leadership abilities enough to prevent federal domination is quite uncertain. A new organization called the Education Commission of the States aims to help the states improve their educational capacities and to present something like a unified front in dealing with the federal government. The commission grew out of James Bryant Conant's suggestion for creating an interstate organization that would make possible a coordinated nationwide policy in American education:

. . . without a drastic Constitutional amendment, nobody is in a position to establish an educational policy in the United

States. It is my contention that some form of cooperative exploration of educational problems between the states and the Federal government is imperative. We cannot have a national educational policy, but we might be able to evolve a *nationwide policy*.[10]

Such an organization came into being in 1966 as the Compact for Education, which in turn created the Education Commission of the States. The commission is made up of senior politicians from many states, including many governors, outstanding laymen, and educators, and it hopes to become the principal means of communication and coordination among the states, and to lead the way in a revitalization of their role in education, particularly in regard to federal-state relations.

It is too early to judge of the commission's success, but the promise is certainly great. Almost all the states have now voluntarily joined the commission and many have done so on far more than a *pro forma* basis. For the first time the United States could have a parliament of the states for education. If vigorously and imaginatively led, it could have a profound effect, and a profoundly healthy one, on our educational system. It could prevent the dissipation of federal funds and meliorate the accumulating power of the United States Office of Education. It could effect badly needed reciprocity among the states in such matters as licensing teachers. It could explore the possibility of guidelines on teachers' salaries. It could be the means of our reaching at last some kind of nationwide policies in such matters as minimum standards and evaluation of educational progress.

Most important of all, perhaps, is the chance that the commission has of finding ways to do what virtually everybody agrees needs doing: making state education departments stronger. But by "stronger" different people mean different things. If the commission merely succeeds in enlarging state departments and getting more money for them to spend, as is already provided for by Title V federal funds, without reforming them in other ways, our problems might simply be compounded. After all, the fundamental weakness of state departments that we explored in

Chapter IV, has been their intellectual vacuity, their lack of leadership, and their devotion to the educational status quo that they have helped to create. These failures will not be cured, but might well be worsened, by making the departments bigger and richer.

The Education Commission of the States got off to an unpromising start. Its chief executive is the former superintendent of schools of Cincinnati and a member in good standing of the professional establishment, which is also well represented on the staff and among the members of the commission. Since its inception the commission has seemed to flounder around a great deal in trying to decide what it should or could do. One of its first publications carried on the front cover a sophomoric cartoon of a jousting match between Thomas W. Braden, then president of the California State Board of Education, and his *bête noire*, Max Rafferty, the state superintendent. In 1967 it organized a conference around the tastelessly contrived theme, "A Power-Play for Control of Education," which seemed to pit the white knights of the states against the black dragon of the federal government in a terminal battle. Perhaps this naïveté will disappear as the commission matures.

On the other hand, there is the very real danger that the commission, like the PTA and the National School Boards Association, will be rendered ineffective through blandness and timidity. The difficulty of adopting policies and programs acceptable to a large and heterogeneous membership is one that many national organizations never overcome. So far the commission has not done so either. Its decision in October 1967 not to participate in the Carnegie national assessment project (which we discussed in Chapter III) nicely points up the commission's dilemma. The assessment project is controversial but highly promising. The commission could well have taken a role in it and might even have been the administrative agent for it without necessarily being contaminated or ideologically committed to the results of the project. But the commission could not take part without offending certain elements of the establishment that have denounced the project *a priori* and that might have been able to make their displeasure known through members of the commission. (Fortunately, this decision is now being re-examined by the commission.)

If the Education Commission of the States is going to be strait-jacketed by the requirements of political or professional compromise, it will probably become just another educational organization, and one whose member states may quickly lose interest. If, however, it is able to surmount these considerable difficulties and face up to the nation's most urgent educational problems, it may well become what it would like to become: the administrative center for the development of interstate and possibly nation-wide policies in education, and the catalyst for a major realignment of authority between the federal government and the states.

On the larger question of this book—whether we can restore a balance of powers generally in American education—I, for one, am fairly optimistic. Our teachers are better educated than in the past and far more aggressive in claiming what they regard as their rights. Administrators are not much better educated but are less aggressive than in the past and are being forced to relinquish some of their power to other persons and groups. Civil rights organizations are a new dimension entirely and promise to give the educational status quo, particularly the big city bureaucracies, a very difficult time. Academic scholars and scientists are much more important in school affairs than they have been for at least half a century.

So all in all, I think our chances are reasonably good of restoring both the teacher and the scholar to a prominent role in educational policy, but not very good for restoring the layman to a position of primacy. Desirable as the latter reform might be, we must face the fact that the main currents of American educational development are flowing mostly away from the ordinary citizen and toward a new coalition of specialists—school administrators, classroom teachers, academicians, federal and state educational officials, along with an assortment of other kinds of specialists (foundation, testing, accrediting, and manufacturing-publishing executives) that I have discussed. Laymen will probably attain a greater voice in inner-city education, but no one can predict with what results; nor is there any reason to think that the lay role will enlarge in other educational areas.

The new order will be better than the old, if for no other reason than the fact that it will be less insular than the old, better educated itself, and more representative of the entire educational community. Even so, laymen would be well advised to keep a sharp eye on it, for it could easily begin to worship its own gods and leave the general public no function whatever except to pay the bills. Ironically, laymen are themselves better educated than in the past and better able to make wise educational policies, but their opportunities for doing so will probably diminish in the future. In order to make or grasp such opportunities, they will need to be more sophisticated than they yet are in the politics of education. I hope this book will be of some help to them.

Appendix

THE EDUCATION LICENSING BOARD OF MASSACHUSETTS

A Proposal for Reconstruction in the Preparation and Certification of Teachers and Administrators for the Public Schools of the State*

"I WANT a man to begin," said Montaigne, "with his conclusions. Grammatical subtleties and an ingenious fabric of words won't do." Acting on that admirable advice, I would like to begin with my conclusion: Massachusetts in the foreseeable future will not be able to staff its public schools with the kind of teachers and administrators that we all say we want unless the present machinery of control is changed.

I don't believe, that is, that any amount of tinkering with the existing mechanism for training and licensing school personnel in this state (or any other state) will produce genuine reform. By "the existing mechanism" I mean not only the present certification laws and procedures, but the established apparatus which governs the preparation of teachers and administrators in our colleges and universities.

I hasten to add that merely changing the machinery will not of itself solve our problems either. It is simply the inescapable prerequisite to an attack on the fundamental question of how to get and keep good teachers and administrators in large numbers throughout the state within a reasonable length of time.

* An address by James D. Koerner to the Advisory Conference on Teacher Education and Certification in Massachusetts, sponsored by the Massachusetts Advisory Council on Education, Boston Massachusetts, February 3, 1968.

It is possible, to be sure, for the Advisory Council's study of teacher education and certification and for the study committee to come up with recommendations that can be carried out within the existing structure of control and that would bring much-needed improvements. We could, for example, raise course requirements for certification beyond their present ludicrous levels; we could reduce the number of credentials to a few basic types; we could endorse the idea of state approval of training programs; we could plump for better practice teaching. We could do these and many similar good deeds and certainly should do them if we are unable to do anything else. But I don't believe that any of them, or all of them together, would assure the schools of the state the kinds of teachers and administrators that are needed now, and certainly in the future.

That infinitely complex job can only be done, if indeed it can be done at all, through the creation of some new instrumentality of control. Such an instrumentality might take any number of forms, and no one is in a position to say what the ideal would be, or if there is one. But I would like to discuss with you the possibilities of a policy-making body different from anything that now exists. For want of a better name, I will call it the Education Licensing Board of Massachusetts.

Before describing this hypothetical entity, let me spend a few minutes talking about the present state of teacher education and why a new method of control is needed. I will try to be restrained and dispassionate in dealing with the always inflammatory subject of what is wrong with teacher education; for I feel that the controversy that has been with us for some years ought now to move beyond the purely partisan stage where colorful combat is often carried on for its own sake and serious discussion is blocked by emotion and unreason. At this point, that is, I have a strong desire to leave old educational battles to history—though not, as Churchill once remarked in Commons—"because I intend to write that history myself." I am content to let others write such histories. But perhaps we could agree on what it is that is chiefly wrong with the present system before we talk about solutions.

The first thing that's wrong are the state's certification laws. The present laws do not protect the public against incompetence; much less are they an incentive to excellence and even less a guarantee of excellence. Moreover, the present laws in Massachusetts and other states are circumvented in a variety of ways, so that some unknown but sizable percentage of teachers in practically all the states is not certified.

The second problem is the lopsided requirements of the training programs themselves. Most of our colleges and universities go far beyond anything the state demands in the way of course credits in education, thereby introducing an imbalance between academic and professional work. If you are in any doubt about this imbalance, let me direct your attention to Chapter 17 of the Willis-Harrington report. It has never been clear to me why so many people in teacher education look only to a change in certification laws or to other action by the states to improve teacher education. It is the preparing institutions themselves that bear a great part of the responsibility for the present situation. Thus I find it hard to get excited about the so-called approved program approach to licensing teachers.

But wholly apart from arithmetical considerations—the courses and hours and units and credits that are taken or not taken by teachers—the much more important fact is that too many teachers continue to come out of training programs poorly prepared for their jobs, *whatever* the reasons, and are fully licensed by the state. The simple but fundamental fact remains that too many elementary teachers emerge from their undergraduate degrees badly educated, with a potpourri of unrelated, unsequential courses in the liberal arts concentrated pretty much in the first two years of college and with vast areas of human knowledge untouched; with an accumulation of repetitious course work in theoretical pedagogy in the last two years; and with practice teaching of highly uncertain quality.

Too many secondary teachers, *whatever* the reasons, come out of their preparatory training unqualified to teach even their major subject, to say nothing of their minor subject, if any, or still other subjects to which they may be misassigned by their administrators. The latest figure to come my way is from the State of Iowa, which has had detailed certification laws for a long time, but which recently found that less than one third of new high school teachers in the state had a college major in the subject they were teaching. In Massachusetts I don't know how much misassignment there is, but I would hazard a guess that it is high even though our licensing standards are low. I also remember a survey made some years ago of school superintendents in Massachusetts in which they listed as their second biggest problem (money was the first problem, of course) the inabilities of their teachers.

Still another big problem, often ignored in discussions of teacher education, is in the graduate school of education. The imbalance between academic and professional study that is common to undergraduate teacher-training programs is far worse at the graduate level, especially in programs for school administrators. This imbalance would not be a problem except for the sheer weight of numbers of administrators in American education—much greater than is found in any other country of the world—and the degree of control they exercise over teachers, over the curriculum, and over many other fundamental matters. The peculiar role that administrators play in our educational system makes their education in turn a matter of pre-eminent concern.

What is wrong with it? The main thing wrong with the customary graduate school program in school administration is, quite simply, its intellectual isolationism. It is wholly concentrated in the school and the faculty of education, just as though the study of economics, politics, history, language and literature, industrial management, public administration, and science and technology—just as though all this had nothing to do with the training of people who want to run the most important institutions of our society. Instead their preparation takes the form of courses in the school of education that are often fragmented, inflated, and pretentious, without a theoretical base or research technique of proven efficacy.

Whenever I contemplate the course requirements for the doctorate in education, I can't help remembering Hildebrand's Law, formulated by Joel Hildebrand, a distinguished professor, chemist, and administrator at the University of California at Berkeley: "The number of courses offered by an academic department is inversely proportional to the intellectual distinction of the faculty and the amount of basic knowledge in the field." Many academic departments, I regret to say, demonstrate the validity of Hildebrand's Law, but the graduate school of education leads all the rest.

I did promise to be both brief and dispassionate, so let's leave the subject by saying that at least we all agree that changes are needed in the education and certification of school personnel in Massachusetts.

Let us then go on to a matter where there may be a substantial measure of disagreement. I believe that if the past proves anything about teacher education, it is that reforms of the scope now needed cannot and will not be made from the inside. They will not come as long as policy-making power is as narrowly concentrated as it is. Anyone who thinks differently ought to ask himself how many of the changes that have been made in teacher education in the last quarter century (and at best there have not been many) have come from inside the industry. Or he might take a look at current documents that represent the collective views of the professional establishment about how to improve teacher education. He might look, for example, at the document produced by the United States Office of Education called *Proposed Standards for State Approval of Teacher Education,* or at such publications of AACTE (the American Association of Colleges for Teacher Education) as its *Standards and Evaluative Criteria for the Accreditation of Teacher Education,* or at the Phi Delta Kappa compilation called *Improving Teacher Education in the United States,* published in 1967, in which a number of forward thinkers from the industry discuss what to them would be a brave new world in teacher education. I don't mean to denigrate these efforts, and indeed I would support some of the positions taken, but the fact is that the kind of change welcomed in these documents is the kind of tame meliorism that one should expect of *any* field not in an advanced stage of decay. It is clear that the teacher-training industry welcomes change if it makes no waves, rocks no boats, usurps no power, unseats no sovereigns, undermines no empires, threatens no financial or professional interests. By all means let there be change, says the establishment, provided it is we who decide the changes.

I may seem to you to be caricaturing the real situation, but I am convinced that the greatest problems in teacher education and certification are created and sustained by a system of control that lacks checks and balances and that has plainly demonstrated an incapacity to reform itself. What I am saying is that the big decisions about how teachers and administrators are trained and licensed are now reposed to far too great a degree in the hands of professional educators, who, after all, represent only one segment of the educational community, not to say the public interest.

The issue of control in teacher education is not complicated. If you believe that an important body of knowledge of proven power exists about how to educate and license teachers and administrators, and that professional educators are in possession of this knowledge while most other people are not, you may want to assign professional educators a dominant voice in the control of training and licensing. If, along with me, you don't believe that such a body of knowledge exists, or if it does that it is not extensive, codified, esoteric, or attainable only through lengthy specialized study, you will, I hope, want to see control more broadly based and more representative.

Either way—whichever of these beliefs is yours—we might still agree that a number of groups in our society have a major stake in the setting of institutional requirements for training, in the establishment of state licensing laws, and in other basic policies. You might, that is, share my belief that teacher training and certification are simply too big and important to be monopolistically controlled. You might also agree that monopolies by definition are dangerous and need to be curbed, even though you and I might not set about trust-busting in the same way.

What voice, for example, do classroom teachers have in teacher education and certification? None whatever. Yet it must be obvious that the views of able and experienced teachers on a great many aspects of the education of a teacher are at least as valuable as those of administrators or members of the education faculty who may not have taught in a school for a decade or two, if ever. I have never understood why the people who run teacher-training programs or establish certification standards fail to give experienced teachers a role in policy deliberations.

It may be that one reason for their failure is that experienced teachers are usually critical of the status quo in teacher education. They manage most of the time to restrain their enthusiasm for certification standards and the teacher-training programs they themselves went through. All attempts that I have ever seen, including some of my own, to find out what teachers think about teacher education—all attempts, that is, that guarantee teachers anonymity or protection from reprisal—bring in results that are as consistent as they are critical.

Unless I badly misread the signs these days, teachers are going to demand and get a much larger voice than they now have in teacher education and certification. They are also going to demand and get a much larger voice in other educational matters on which they have rarely been consulted in the past. No matter what we do here or what the results of the Advisory Council's study, it seems clear to me that Massachusetts teachers are going to have something to say in the future about their own training and about licensing. I, for one, look forward to the change. But I would also admit that my many hopes in this matter are conditioned by a few fears. My main fear is that teachers will subordinate excellence in training and licensing to the predominate concerns of their professional organizations with salaries. My main hope is that they will find a way to harmonize both objectives.

Another group with a big stake but no voice in the education of teachers and administrators is the people who hire and pay them—the laymen, currently over 100,000 of them, who serve on school boards and provide a living for over two million teachers and administrators. Again it has always seemed odd to me that the people who must evaluate and employ in such large numbers those who come out of educational training programs should have no voice in these programs or in licensing requirements. Nor is there even provisions for feedback from employers of school personnel to training institutions.

Still another group that has been disfranchised in the government of teacher education is the faculty of arts and sciences in our colleges and universities. The liberal arts departments in a given institution may have some control over students in that institution who are preparing to teach academic subjects at the secondary level, but their control may well be limited to the setting of majors and minors. In many institutions, probably most, they have nothing to say about the rest of the education their prospective teachers receive, nothing to say about general policy in teacher education, nothing to say about the preparation of elementary school teachers, nothing at all to say about the education of school administrators, and nothing whatever to say about state certification requirements.

The "all-institutional" approach to teacher education may work reasonably well in some liberal arts colleges and a few universities, but it is mere window dressing in many other institutions and nonexistent in many more. Neither through their individual institutions nor through their professional associations do the people who know the most about the subjects that make up the bulk of the school curriculum—English, history, foreign languages, mathematics, biology, chemistry, and physics—enjoy any significant policy-making functions in teacher education and licensing.

Fortunately this situation is also beginning to change. The curriculum reform movement that began with Max Beberman and his mathematics group at the University of Illinois and with MIT's Physical Science Study Committee has expanded beyond anything that could have been imagined a decade ago. Major reform work is now going forward in almost all of the basic school subjects through the collaboration of outstanding scholars and classroom teachers. The result has been a revitalization of large parts of the curriculum and the reinvolvement of the academic community, at least a part of it, in public school affairs.

So far the influence of the curriculum reform groups on teacher education has been confined to in-service institutes of great variety and differing quality. Not much headway has yet been made in pre-service programs and none whatever in certification standards. However, it seems a safe prediction that the influence of this movement on regular teacher-training programs will soon begin to grow. Even more important is the fact that there now exists a large nucleus of first-rate scholars who have a lasting interest in, and an extensive experience with, public education. They might well be the group through which the voice of the academic community can be re-established in teacher education and certification, especially in Massachusetts where so much curriculum reform work has been done. Still, this broadening of participation in the control of teacher education on the part of relatively few scholars and teachers is quite isolated. It is sporadic, not organized, and certainly not nationwide or even statewide.

I would ask you, then, to speculate with me about what sort of body could be created to generate and sustain reform in the training and licensing of teachers and administrators. How can we prevent the monopolization of power by one interest group? How can we bring disfranchised groups into some kind of federation that will preserve a balance of powers? How can we create an instrumentality that will reassert state leadership and at the same time be able to adjust continuously to rapidly changing educational conditions, including conditions that at some point in the future might call for its own disestablishment?

It might be done in a dozen different ways. The State Board of Education could possibly begin to exercise the authority given it over teacher education and certification by the Willis-Harrington Act. It might, for example, put some advisory committees to work that are representative of the major interests involved in teacher education and might try to change our licensing laws on the basis of their recommendations. But the state board is very busy on other fronts and will probably continue to be for some time. Even if it were able to give the problem some concentrated attention, it would not be able to give teacher education and certification the kind of long-term continuous attention it needs.

Or conceivably the State Department of Education could organize some sort of broadly based group and charge it with preparing a reform plan in teacher education and certification that the commissioner might then try to sell to the state board or to the legislature. But educational organizations are rarely good at introspective analysis, and educators with a large stake in established procedures that they themselves helped to create over the years are no more likely than businessmen or politicians or labor unions to be enthusiastic about changing the rules. State departments of education, perhaps in the nature of things, are not often found in the vanguard of educational reform.

Although neither I nor anybody else knows what the best way might be of solving the multitudinous problems of teacher education, I hope you will consider one that seems promising to me. Let me describe it in rough outline only. I want, that is, to talk, not about the reform of teacher education or certification, but about creating a *means* for generating reform. The Willis-Harrington Commission decided early in its deliberations that it could not spell out all the reforms needed in Massachusetts education, that such a job was too big and complex for the time and money available to the commission. Instead, it wisely decided to address itself to the problem of how to create a system of control in the state that in turn would identify and institute the reforms needed. Perhaps we are at the same point in teacher education and certification. So I now want to talk with you about means rather than ends.

Suppose the legislature were to establish a new state authority; call it the Education Licensing Board of Massachusetts. Sup-

pose we put it under the State Board of Education, as I have indicated on the diagram that appears later, but give it full
authority over the certification of school personnel. Suppose, that
is, we interposed it between the State Board of Education and the
Department of Education, whose Certification Bureau would
continue its customary administrative functions. I see no contradiction in a body that is independent but under the state board.
There is legislative language that covers the matter: the state
board itself is "in but not under" the Department of Education.
The licensing board that I am proposing could be "in but not
under" the state board. I want to stress its freedom, for a body
that was merely advisory would probably not work in Massachusetts, any more than advisory bodies now in existence in other
states are effective in the reform of teacher education and certification.

The Massachusetts Licensing Board might be made up of, say,
fifteen persons drawn from the ranks of three groups: (1) experienced classroom teachers; (2) outstanding members of college and
university faculties—whether professional educators, or scholars
and academicians with a demonstrated interest in public education; and (3) distinguished laymen drawn possibly from local
school boards. The board might also have *ex officio* or other kinds
of representation, but the three groups I have named would constitute the major part of the board. There would be no spokesmen for teacher-training programs or for the teacher education
industry as such, any more than local school districts are represented as such on the State Board of Education.

Nor would academic subjects or fields as such be represented.
The membership, in other words, would be made up of outstanding persons whose distinction happens to be in certain fields or
endeavors and who share a devotion to education. But no one
would be there as a spokesman for his speciality. Such a board
would, I believe, bring into the governing of teacher education
and certification a balance of powers that is not possible in the
present system.

How board membership was determined would be the quintessential problem—for the board's success would obviously turn on the kinds of people serving on it. How do we avoid electing or appointing teachers to such a board who may be excellent in the classroom and well known among the state's teachers but who are interested only in the narrower aspects of teacher power? How do we avoid getting professional educators who are hostile to the whole enterprise and want either to control or neutralize the board's authority? How do we avoid academics who think only in terms of their own subject or who know little about public education? How do we avoid laymen who are known and respected by everybody but who serve on the board only to become still better known and respected? I don't know. But I am confident that the problem is soluble if the idea of the board itself is acceptable.

It may be that the legislature would decide to control appointments to the board, with, one hopes, the obvious safeguards against purely political appointments. Or the governor might appoint the members from lists of people submitted to him, perhaps by the Advisory Council. The council in turn might confer with the appropriate professional and scholarly state and national groups. Possibly some appointments could be made from the Massachusetts members of such notable bodies as the National Academy of Sciences or the American Philosophical Society. In any case, I am confident that the problem of selection could be solved if it were recognized from the beginning as critical.

If such a board were brought into existence, one of the first decisions it might make was that it was not able by itself to establish detailed regulations for the licensing of many different kinds of teachers and administrators. No one should underestimate the complexity of the issues with which the board would have to deal or the difficulties that any single body would face in reconstructing the state's system of training and licensing school personnel.

Suppose the board, in its becoming modesty, decided to create under itself a series of units that I will arbitrarily call panels, which would advise the board on detailed regulations. There might be a panel, for example, for each of the principal subjects of the school curriculum or for related groups of subjects. There might be a history panel, a mathematics panel, a foreign languages panel, etc. The panels might be made up of five or seven or nine persons divided between scholars and classroom teachers of the subjects involved. The panels might have only advisory authority but one's strong expectation would be that the board would follow their advice; possibly their authority could be more than advisory.

The job of the panels, quite simply, would be to keep the board continuously apprised of training and licensing needs in their subject. They would need to stay abreast of the supply-demand situation in their subject; they would have to worry about misassignment; they would have to decide how teachers of their subject should be licensed by the state. Obviously these panels would not move in splendid isolation of one another or of the training institutions themselves, but they might come up with anything but homogeneous requirements. Standards, that is, might easily differ from subject to subject.

Let's consider for a moment how one of the panels might operate. Suppose we take for illustration a universal subject, say English. The Licensing Board talks to such bodies as the Massachusetts branch of the National Council of Teachers of English and perhaps to the Modern Language Association, as well as to anybody else whose opinions it values in the matter, and winds up appointing or having appointed a panel of seven people for high school English: four scholars who have evidenced their interest in and knowledge of public education and who perhaps have been involved in curriculum reform, and three outstanding teachers of English from the schools.

The panel meets and decides that before it makes recommendations to the Licensing Board it would like to find out who now teaches English in Massachusetts schools. It puts the data processing equipment of the Department of Education to work and discovers to its horror that half the people teaching high school English in the state's public schools have neither a major nor any other significant preparation in the subject. (Let me in passing remind you that our present licensing laws state that "A secondary school teacher may not devote more than 50 percent of teaching time to subjects in which he or she is not qualified to teach as a major." Since a teacher is "qualified" in Massachusetts with eighteen semester hours, the regulation means that he can spend half of his time teaching physics or mathematics, for example, in our high schools if he has had nine semester hours in that subject—and that's nine hours from any college under any instructor at any time in the past.)

The panel also discovers that many of those with a major in English have glaring gaps in their preparation, that they have had perhaps no work in advanced grammar, advanced composition, linguistics, the phonetic alphabet, or the history of the language. The panel also discovers that there is really no way, anyhow, of evaluating, equating, or comparing the paper credits of one teacher with another because of the multiplicity of preparing institutions, programs, and standards. The panel decides that it really can't assume that six credit hours in "English Literature of the Seventeenth Century" taken at an impoverished state college under a professor who himself has a master's degree in Twentieth Century American Literature from a minor institution in the south is entirely equal to a year of work in that subject from say Harvard's Douglas Bush. Yet that is precisely what our certification laws now assume.

But it's an imperfect world and our anguished panel decides to be both realistic and bold. It regretfully decides that it can't for the present escape the quantitative trap and decides to continue to license English teachers on the basis of degree data. Conceivably it might *not* decide that; it might find a new procedure entirely. But let's say it decides that the minimum for full licensing hereafter will be a substantial major of perhaps forty semester hours that includes work in certain areas of the subject it knows are needed by teachers.

It finds that most of the English departments around the state approve of its recommendations and are anxious to cooperate; they know the deficiencies but have been busy frying other fish.

The panel would *like* to experiment with a two-level system of licensure for English teachers tied to an advanced degree that is approved by the Licensing Board or perhaps to a combination of advanced work and a record of proven accomplishment in teaching. But it doubts that teachers organizations in their present state of evolution are ready to buy such a plan, and decides to work quietly behind the scenes for a while and see if professional support can be crystallized around that or a better idea.

Meanwhile it takes care to avoid substituting new rigidities for old. It recognizes that many communities in Massachusetts might be lucky enough to have people in residence who have distinguished themselves in literature, journalism, or other kinds of writing but who might never have sat in a college English class, not to say an education class. Or there might be in residence a number of former teachers from private schools or from foreign countries or from institutions of higher education. The panel therefore says that it stands ready to license *anybody* on the basis of achievement in the subject and hopes that the schools of the state will make an effort to lure people into their classrooms either full time or part time who might not fit neatly into the customary mold. It might even say that it stands ready to license anybody on the basis of examination or other criteria even though they may never have taught; it might, that is, decide to license people sometimes on the basis of faith, as is often the case now with fully certified teachers.

Reminded, perhaps by the lay members of the Licensing Board, of some harsh facts of economics and manpower supply, the panel for English also recognizes that the English classrooms of the state's high schools will not all be filled with teachers of the required background and ability in a short time, and makes the appropriate adjustments in its recommendations to the Licensing Board about emergency measures. But it holds firm to its basic position that no new teachers will be fully licensed without meeting the panel's established standards.

Other panels might behave in quite different ways. In subjects where a teacher's knowledge and technique are more or less measurable, at least for purposes of maintaining a definable qualitative standard, the panels might well decide to include examinations in their licensing procedure. The panel for foreign languages might, as I would hope, require a written and oral examination for licensing; for that indeed is the common sense requirement that has been supported for a long time by the Massachusetts Foreign Languages Association, an agency that, one hopes, would be represented on the foreign languages panel. The mathematics panel might decide that some concrete demonstration of a teacher's grasp of mathematics is essential for licensing. The panels in science might require laboratory demonstrations or other evidence of ability. The social studies panel, if there were one, might decide . . . God knows what.

The chief virtue of these panels is, quite simply, that they provide the Licensing Board with a means whereby continuous attention can be given to teacher preparation and certification in each subject by a body of people that brings expertise, practical experience, and advanced scholarship to the task.

The Licensing Board might reserve certain specialties for its own attention. Rather than have a panel on requirements for elementary school teachers, for instance, it might want to tackle that complicated problem itself. It might also want to reserve for its own attention the requirements for administrative and nonteaching personnel. In its politic wisdom it might decide to avoid an open battle with NCATE or the ASSA, or with orthodox advanced-degree programs of the schools of education. On the other hand, it might decide that such a battle really had to be faced, in which case I, for one, would loudly applaud.

The board would also be a far more flexible means of dealing with special problems than is the existing machinery. It might, for example, experiment with quite unorthodox methods of getting and keeping good teachers in the inner-city schools, since this problem is not being solved and cannot be solved with orthodox methods. It might try working with New York's new Urban Teachers Corps, for example, to see if some of our own inner-city problems can be solved.

It might try to open up several avenues, or a great many avenues, to the teaching license instead of just one. It might want to promote some experiments in full-time, school-based internships. It might want to make special licensing provisions for veterans of the Peace Corps, VISTA, the Job Corps, the armed services, or for other people with specialized experience. It might want to make special provisions to license scientists, artists, musicians, poets, or anybody else with a record of achievement that local schools might be able to tempt into the classroom.

It might want to think about the possibilities of establishing some kind of senior qualification for teachers of experience and accomplishment—a license with some prestige that might be based on competitive examinations or on demonstrated accomplishment in teaching or on both; something similar, perhaps, to "board-certified" medical specialists or perhaps to the coveted French status of *agrégé*. It might want to try yielding full autonomy to train and hire teachers to a few pilot school districts, allowing them to go about staffing their schools in any way they chose. It might try yielding autonomy to selected institutions of higher education to conduct their training programs in any way they chose. Quite possibly it might authorize other kinds of institutions such as Education Development Center, the regional educational laboratory in the New England area, to undertake some teacher-training experiments of their own.

It might also want to put the weight of its influence behind the "new curricula," and encourage institutions to construct their teacher-training programs so that people coming out of them are able to handle the new courses of study and do not have to be immediately retrained. Or it might undertake to persuade the Office of Education's big new bureau on teacher education that the "innovative" programs which the office says it is looking for do not always and ever have to be found in, or be conducted in, institutions of higher education. Maybe the board could help shake the teacher-training folk in the Office of Education out of what John Stuart Mill once called "the deep slumber of accepted opinion," and persuade them to back, say, a radical school-based or community-based training program in Roxbury or in a rural area of western Massachusetts.

But, you might say, the plan is full of unanswered questions. What about reciprocity, for instance? What if such a Licensing Board established standards that could not be met by teachers coming from other states? What about the regional or nationwide reciprocity arrangements already developing with NCATE, or with the New England states, or with the Education Commission of the States?

Or you might ask what the board would do about small rural districts that could not begin to pay enough money to get the kind of teachers or administrators we have been talking about. Or you might ask why anybody should think that such a board would be any better at enforcing whatever standards it enunciated than is the present system.

Or you might ask how the board would cope with such impending challenges as educational technology. Although the great hopes and claims of the last fifteen or twenty years for electronic education have yet to come to fruition, we have heard some startling projections about the future impact of technology on education in general and therefore on teacher education. We heard some surprising predictions about what education would be like in 1980—or was it 1984?—with teachers who may be ringmasters of a kind, who would no longer need to have much in their heads because it would all be in the computer. If such predictions turn out to be true, you might ask, how would the Licensing Board cope with that apocalyptic revolution?

The answer, of course, is that I don't know how the board would resolve these and lots of other problems. And I don't want to worry about them. I want *the board* to worry about them. But I am confident that this board or something like it would be a much more effective way of dealing with our problems in teacher education and certification, present and future, than we have now in any of the states. The board would be a much more supple instrument, more adaptive, more responsive, more representative, and much more respected than anything that now exists.

To many of you the plan may have one big flaw; it tends to centralize rather than distribute power over teacher education and certification at a time when James Bryant Conant and lots of other people are plumping for what they call "institutional autonomy" or the approved-program approach. I would answer this important objection by reminding you again that the chief reason people are now enamored of institutional autonomy in teacher education is the record of weakness and lack of leadership on the part of the states, and not really the fear of centralized control. It is precisely because the states have failed to exert their authority—have failed to carry out their responsibilities to insure well qualified staff to the public schools—that Conant and others now want to shift these responsibilities to the individual institutions.

But unfortunately the record strongly suggests that institutional autonomy is not going to solve the problems. As I have already pointed out, institutional autonomy is what, in effect, we have had for a great many years, or at least freedom from state domination, though not freedom from national organizations that call themselves "voluntary" groups. Most institutions that prepare teachers and administrators have for a long, long time gone far beyond anything required by the states for certification. They have, in other words, trained school personnel in more or less the way they wanted to train them. Rarely have they been frustrated, and even more rarely hamstrung, by state laws.

How effective, then, has been this institutional autonomy? Alas, if it had been effective, you and I would not be foregathered here today to talk about reform in teacher education and certification. I therefore readily grant that the Licensing Board does represent a degree of centralized control. That indeed is the whole idea. To put the matter bluntly, I don't think we are yet at the point where the states can trust most of the institutions to turn out good people. But please remember that the Licensing Board has the power to do so—that it can elect to trust the institutions—at any time it decides that certain colleges or universities are ready not merely to demand freedom but to accept responsibility for results. Meanwhile, the *raison d'être* of the Licensing Board is to reclaim the authority of the state in the education and certification of personnel for the public schools.

Or the board might seem to you something that only a lover of administration and organization could conjure up. I should be sorry indeed if you felt that way, since my instincts are all in the other direction. I don't think the board would be either expensive or administratively cumbersome. Still, as I indicated at the beginning, the addition of the Licensing Board to the extensive and convoluted machinery of state government would not of itself insure success. For all its good intentions and firm resolutions, it would not, after all, automatically improve the quality of a single training program. One can even imagine the board in full operation but with the general level of teacher education remaining about where it is. Such dismal possibilities are probably inherent in all educational schemes, but I think they are minimal in this one.

Still, my proposal no doubt has plenty of bugs. Grand new plans for education have a way of falling on their face, either because their high-flying inventors overlook fatal flaws that are plain to other people, or because visionary plans are actually adopted and prove immediately hopeless in action. I don't think that is the case with the Licensing Board, but I am willing to admit the possibility.

As you see, I have not tried to anticipate all the problems that could arise if the board were created. So I hope you won't reject the whole proposal because you see imperfections in it. The guts of the plan are in the broad interests and balance of powers represented on the board and in the specialized panels that operate under it. I hope that Massachusetts, a state that was exceedingly slow to institute any kind of state certification, will now lead the way for many other states in reforming the whole structure of teacher education and licensing.

MASSACHUSETTS STATE BOARD OF EDUCATION

THE EDUCATION LICENSING BOARD OF MASSACHUSETTS
(classroom teachers—scholars, academicians, professionals—laymen)

Certification
Bureau of
State Department
of Education

Subject
panel-
(scholars
and
teachers)

Subject
panel

Subject
panel

Subject
panel

Subject
panel

Subject
panel

Notes

Foreword

1. Terry Ferrer, "Conant Revisited," *Saturday Review*, March 18, 1967, p. 73.

Chapter I

1. Founders Day Banquet speech, Washington University, February 25, 1967.

2. Roscoe C. Martin, *The Cities and the Federal System*, Atherton, 1965, p. 26.

3. "Federal Education, Training, and Related Programs" (Special Analysis G), Bureau of the Budget, 1967, p. 93.

4. Joseph Justman, "The Government and the Schools," *School and Society*, February 4, 1967, p. 76.

5. Stephen K. Bailey, *The Office of Education and the Education Act* (Inter-University Case Program #100), Bobbs-Merrill, 1966, p. 19.

Chapter II

1. Nicholas A. Masters, Robert H. Salisbury, and Thomas H. Eliot, *State Politics and the Public Schools*, Knopf, 1964, p. 271.

2. Myron Lieberman and Michael H. Moskow, *Collective Negotiations for Teachers*, Rand McNally, 1966, pp. 169–171 and 404–405.

3. From his inaugural speech, October 20, 1967, Washington, D.C.

Chapter III

1. Donald Barr, "The Little Gold Schoolhouse," *Book Week*, October 30, 1966, p. 3.

2. Maintenance of Academic Standards through Accreditation in the United States of America," undated (1966?), p. 7.

3. *The Comprehensive High School; A Second Report to Interested Citizens*, McGraw-Hill, 1967, p. 55.

4. *The Foundation Directory*, 3rd edition, Russell Sage Foundation, 1967, p. 9.

5. Here, for example, is the way reading experts are apt to define their speciality: "Reading is a processing skill of symbolic reasoning sustained by the interfacilitation of an intricate hierarchy of substrata factors that have been mobilized as a psychological working system and pressed into service in accordance with the purpose of the reader." Teachers in training no doubt assume that such a statement has meaning, but perhaps the best response to it is a comment that Harold Howe, II, United States Commissioner of Education, made recently: "Educators have often been accused of developing a polysyllabic gibberish intelligible to them alone. I think we must not dismiss such complaints as minor and unimportant peeves; language is too closely tied to thought for us to regard our choice of words as a trivial matter. George Orwell maintained—and I think he made a sound case for his proposition— that the quality of a nation's political debate affects the quality of its politics. Words are not merely the vehicle of thought; they *are* the thought, and an idea poorly expressed by an educator is, quite simply, a poor or garbled idea."

Chapter IV

1. Nicholas A. Masters, Robert H. Salisbury, and Thomas H. Eliot, *State Politics and the Public Schools*, Knopf, 1964, p. 7.

2. "Federal Financial Relationships to Education," National Education Association, 1967.

3. George D. Marconnit, "School Legislatures and the School Curriculum," *Phi Delta Kappan*, January 1968, pp. 269 and 272.

4. "The Tangled Web; Final Report of the Assembly Interim Committee on Education," January 1967, Sacramento, pp. 10 and 13.

5. Quoted by B. Dean Bowles, *Educational Pressure Groups and the Legislative Process in California, 1945–1966,* unpublished doctoral dissertation at the Claremont Graduate School, Claremont, California, 1966, p. 137.

6. Ewald B. Nyquist (Deputy Commissioner of Education, New York State), in a speech to the Conference on the Emerging Role of State Departments of Education, Columbus, Ohio, 1967.

7. *Shaping Educational Policy*, McGraw-Hill, 1964, pp. 37–38.

8. *Reinforcing the Role of the States in Education; The Second Annual Report of the Advisory Council on State Departments of Education,* United States Office of Education, March 1967, p. 19.

9. *A New Organizational System for State-Level Educational Administrations; A Recommended Response to Emerging Requirements for Change in California,* report to the California State Board of Education by Arthur D. Little, Inc., Cambridge, Massachusetts, 1967.

10. Speech at the Midwestern Governors' Conference, Mackinac Island,

Michigan, September 21, 1965. A good short statement of Sanford's ideas is his "New Era Ahead for Your State," *Nation's Business*, July 1965, pp. 56–64.

11. *Storm Over the States*, McGraw-Hill, 1967.

12. Nicholas A. Masters, Robert H. Salisbury, and Thomas H. Eliot, *State Politics and the Public Schools*, Knopf, 1964, pp. 268–269.

13. Harmon Zeigler, *The Political World of the High School Teacher*, Center for the Advanced Study of Educational Administration, University of Oregon, 1966, p. 54.

14. "Report of the Joint Interim Committee on the Public Education System," Senate of the State of California, 1961, p. 5.

15. *Teacher Supply and Demand in California, 1965–1975*, Arthur D. Little, Inc., Cambridge, Massachusetts, February 1967.

16. *The Restoration of Teaching*, Report of the Subcommittee on School Personnel and Teacher Qualifications of the Assembly Interim Committee on Education, p. 13.

17. *Report of the Special Commission Established to Make an Investigation and Study Relative to Improving and Extending Educational Facilities in the Commonwealth*, House Document #4300, Boston, Massachusetts, June 1965.

18. In February 1968 the Massachusetts commissioner resigned, effective at the end of the year. In May 1967 he had been attacked by the *Globe* for ineffective leadership and in October 1967 by the Massachusetts Education Association, which accused him of being out of touch with contemporary educational movements, but he rejected any suggestion at the time of his resignation that his action was connected in any way with this or any other criticism.

Chapter V

1. Harvey Pressman, *New Schools for the Cities*, New Community Press, 1967, p. 8.

2. "Profiles in Excellence; Recommended Criteria for Evaluating the Quality of a Local School System," National Education Association, 1966.

3. Keith Goldhammer, *The School Board*, Center for Applied Research, New York, New York, 1964, p. 76.

4. "School Board Members' Reactions to Educational Innovations," Gallup International, Inc., November 1966, pp. 7–8. The survey was commissioned by the Institute for the Development of Educational Activities.

5. *School Boards and School Board Membership*, Report of the New York State Regents Advisory Committee on Educational Leadership, 1966, pp. 1 and 50.

6. Harry B. Gilbert, *et al.*, *Teacher Selection Policies and Procedures in Large Public School Systems in the United States*, Board of Education of the City of New York, 1966, p. 19.

7. *Education News*, October 30, 1967, pp. 1 and 14.

8. *Education, U. S. A.,* October 30, 1967, p. 49.

9. Dick Netzer, *Economics of the Property Tax,* Brookings Institution, 1966, pp. 1, 3, and 117.

10. Stephen K. Bailey, in *Schoolmen and Politics,* Syracuse University Press, 1962, p. 103.

11. *The Comprehensive High School; A Second Report to Interested Citizens,* McGraw-Hill, 1967, pp. 19–20.

12. Roland J. Pellegrin, "Community Power Structure and Educational Decision-Making in the Local Community," a paper presented at the 1965 convention of the American Association of School Administrators, Atlantic City, February 15, 1965.

13. Marilyn Gittell, *Participants and Participation; A Study of School Policy in New York City,* Center for Urban Education, 1967, pp. 46, 48, and 54.

14. John F. Gallagher, *Decision Making in Public Education,* Occasional Paper Series No. 5, Institute of Government Affairs, University of California (Davis), 1965, pp. 33, 44–45, and 52.

15. Ralph B. Kimbrough, *Political Power and Educational Decision-Making,* Rand McNally, 1964, p. 271.

16. Keith Goldhammer, *et al., Issues and Problems in Contemporary Educational Administration,* Center for the Advanced Study of Educational Administration, University of Oregon, 1967, pp. 3–4.

17. *School Boards and School Board Membership; Report of the New York State Regents Advisory Committee on Educational Leadership,* 1965, pp. 58–59.

18. David W. Minar, in *The Politics of Education in the Local Community, Interstate Printers,* 1964, pp. 1 and 141.

19. Keith Goldhammer, *et al., Issues and Problems in Contemporary Educational Administration,* Center for the Advanced Study of Educational Administration, University of Oregon, 1967, pp. 31–32.

20. *Chief Education Officers; Recommendation and Report of a Survey by the New York State Regents Advisory Committee on Educational Leadership,* 1966, pp. 2–3.

21. Robert A. Dahl, *Who Governs?* Yale University Press, 1961, p. 152.

22. "Let Us Teach; Final Report on the Helpfulness of Certain Aspects of the School Program to Classroom Teaching," the Senate Fact-finding Committee on Governmental Administration, 1965, p. 8.

23. Richard F. Carter, *Voters and Their Schools,* Institute for Communication Research, Stanford University, 1960, pp. 135 and 162.

24. Robert A. Dahl, *Who Governs?* Yale University Press, 1961, p. 156.

25. Robert Presthus, *Men at the Top,* Oxford University Press, 1964, p. 405.

26. Neal Gross, *Who Runs Our Schools?* John Wiley, 1958, pp. 6 and 34.

27. *Chief School Officers; Recommendations and Report of a Survey by the New York State Regents Advisory Committee on Educational Leadership,* 1966, pp. 88–91.

28. David W. Minar, *Educational Decision-Making in Suburban Communities*, Cooperative Research Project No. 2440 (mimeographed), Northwestern University, 1966, p. 8.

29. Louis H. Masotti, *Education and Politics in Suburbia*, Press of Western Reserve University, 1967, p. 66.

Chapter VI

1. In an address to the Harvard Summer School Conference on Educational Administration, July 14, 1966.

2. Robert H. Salisbury, in *Planning for a Nation of Cities*, MIT Press, 1966, p. 271.

3. Jeanne S. Chall, *Learning to Read; The Great Debate*, McGraw-Hill, 1967.

4. "The Antileadership Vaccine," in *The Annual Report of the Carnegie Corporation, 1965*, p. 8.

5. *Shaping Educational Policy*, McGraw-Hill, 1964, p. 29.

6. Sidney C. Sufrin, *Issues in Federal Aid to Education*, Syracuse University Press, 1962, p. 20.

7. Alan K. Campbell and Philip Meranto, "The Metropolitan Education Dilemma," *Urban Affairs Quarterly*, September 1966, p. 62.

8. Joseph A. Pechman, *Federal Tax Policy*, Brookings Institution, 1966, p. 203.

9. Testimony before the Senate Committee on Government Operations, November 18, 1966.

10. *Shaping Educational Policy*, McGraw-Hill, 1964, p. 110.

Index

Accrediting associations: 51-59; influence of, 54-55; regional, 55
Adams, Arthur S.: 109
Administrators: power of local: 137-146
Advanced placement tests: 49
AFL-CIO: 78
African Education Program: 63
American Association of Colleges for Teacher Education: 57, 179
American Association of School Administrators: 38, 43, 58, 69, 137, 148
American Association of University Professors: 26, 43
American Chemical Society: 60
American College Testing Program: 49-50
American Council on Education: 109
American Federation of Teachers: 26-45, 145; budget of, 29; headquarters of, 30; policies of, 30-45; and state legislatures, 33; publications of, 34; recent gains of, 35; and NEA, 35-36, 38, 41, 43; and administrators, 38-41; and segregation, 41; and states, 99
American Philosophical Society: 186

American Telephone and Telegraph: 76
Appalachian Regional Commission: 19
Arkansas: 119
Atomic Energy Commission: 19, 20

Baker v. Carr: 7
Barnard, Henry: 9
Beberman, Max: 60, 182
Bell and Howell: 76
"Big Six": 148
Biological Sciences Curriculum Study: 60
Biology: and reform groups, 60
Boston Globe: 106, 107, 113, 199
Boston School Committee: 114-115
Braden, Thomas W.: 172
Brown v. Board of Education of Topeka: 6
Bundy, McGeorge: 132
Burroughs: 75
Bush, Douglas: 188
Butler, Nicholas Murray: 34

California: 85, 86, 143, 144, 165; legislature and education, 81-82; state board of education in, 88-91, 172; state education department, 91, 93-94; Master Plan for

Higher Education, 109; school boards in, 126
California, University of: 60
California, University of Southern: 128
California Citizens Advisory Commission: 103, 117
California Council on Teacher Education: 105
California Teachers Association: 82, 98, 105
Canada: 120
Carnegie Corporation: 66
Carnegie Foundation: 66-69
Carr, William: 43
CBS: 76
Chamber of Commerce: 78
Chemical Bond Approach Project: 60
Chemical Education Material Study: 60
Chemistry: and reform groups, 60
Chicago: 120, 123
Christian Science Monitor: 78
CIA: 19
Citizens advisory groups: 70-78
Civil Rights Act (1964), Title VI: 11
Civil Rights Movement: 132, 154, 173
Cleveland: Catholic institutions in, 121
Coleman report: 21
Collective bargaining: 145-146; growth of, 42
"Collective negotiations": 37-38
College boards: and national exams, 48-49
College Entrance Examination Board: 48
Colorado: 39
Columbia University. See Teachers College

Commission on Civil Rights: 21
Commission on Educational Television: 66
Commission on Law Enforcement and Administration of Justice: 21-22
Committee for Economic Development: 78
Committee on Assessing the Progress of Education: 66
"Community Counseling Kits": 73
Compact for Education: 66, 171
Conant, James Bryant: 58, 76, 102, 108, 193; on political action, viii-ix; on new courses in high schools, 65; and Education Commission of the States, 83; on state departments of education, 92-93; on school finance, 136; on "establishment," 163-164; on education policy in U.S., 170-171
Cooperative Extension Service: 20
Cooperative Research Program: 16
Council for Basic Education: 58, 73-74, 159; Bulletin, 73-74, 165
Council of Chief State School Officers: 87, 94, 148
"Council on College-Level Examinations": 51
County school boards: 119-120
Curriculum reform groups: 59-65

Decentralization of schools: 132
Delaware: 135
Derthick, Lawrence G.: 35
Desegregation of schools: 7-8
Detroit: 120
District of Columbia: 131
Donahue, Maurice A.: 108
Driver training: 153

Economic Opportunity Act of 1964: 5

Education: politics of, viii; and federal government, 3-24; and Congress, 4-6; and judicial branch, 6-8; and publishing industry, 74-75; and religious groups, 76-77; and mass media, 77-78; and state government, 79-117; and local control, 118-154; and parents, 146-154; and the public, 150; role of layman in, 166
Education Act (1965): 167
Education Commission of the States: 83, 170, 171, 172, 173, 192
Education Development Center: 15, 64, 191
Education News: 133
"Education Parks": 21
Education Program Message of Congress, January 1965: quoted, 14
Education Services, Inc.: 63
Education U.S.A.: 134
"Educationalist": 15
Educational Policies Commission: 34
Educational Services, Inc.: 13, 15
Educational technology: 75-76, 192
Educational Testing Service, Princeton, N.J.: 48, 128, 161
"Educationist": 15
Educators. *See* Professional educators
Eisenhower, D.D.: 35
Elementary and Secondary Education Act of 1965: 5; Title IV, 13; Title V, 93
Elementary School Science Project: 60
Elementary Science Study: 60
Encyclopaedia Britannica: 76
England: 120, 137, 149; National Union of Teachers, 39; school boards in, 123-124; power of teachers in, 144
English: teaching of, 187-189

Equality of Educational Opportunity: 21
"Establishment": defined, 31
Europe: and education ministries, 8; teachers associations in, 39-40; national exams in, 47
Executive branch: and education, 19-22

Farm Bureau: 78
Federal courts: 7
Federal government: and education, 3-24; expenditure for education, 21; indirect influence on educational policy, 21-22; improvement of educational operations, 23; power in education, 23; and education in future, 24; aid to education and states' rights position, 167; its money and states, 168-169
Finances, school: 134-135
Fischer, John H.: 84
Fisher Act: 82, 104, 105
Flemming, Arthur S.: 35
Flesch, Rudolf: 158
Florida: and NEA sanctions, 37
Florida Education Association: 98-99
Ford Foundation: 66, 132
Forman, Ian: 106, 107, 113
Foundations: 65-70
France: 46, 137; education ministry in, 8; *Association des Agrégés*, 40
Froude, James A.: 118

Gallup poll: on school boards, 125
Gardner, John W.: 13, 67, 160, 163; quoted, 3-4, 169-170
General Dynamics: 76
General Electric: 75
George-Barden Act of 1946: 5
GI Bill of Rights: 5
Goodyear: 76

Government. *See* Federal government; State government
Great Britain: 8-9, 46
Gross National Product: 21, 169
"Guide for the Evaluation of Institutions of Higher Education": 56

Harrington, Kevin B.: 108, 112, 113, 116, 117
Harvard University, Graduate School of Education: 127-128
Harvey Mudd College: 60
Hawaii: 81
Head Start: 20
High schools, public: accrediting of, 53-54
Higher Education Act of 1965: 5
Hildebrand, Joel: 179
Hildebrand's Law: 179
Howe, Harold II: 163, 198; quoted, 157
Hugo, Victor: 71

IBM: 14, 75
Illinois: 33, 96, 102, 119
Illinois, University of: 60, 182
Illinois Citizens' Committee for Teacher Education: 102
Improving Teacher Education in the United States: 179
Indiana: 85, 120
"Interstate Compact for Education": 83
Iowa: 85, 96, 178
Italy: education ministry in, 8

Job Corps: 20, 191
Johns Hopkins University, Applied Physics Laboratory: 20
Johnson, L.B.: and regional labs, 14
Joint Interim Committee on the Public Education System: 103

Judicial branch: and education, 6-8

Kansas: 96, 118
Kellogg Foundation: 70
Kennedy, John F.: 35
Keppel, Francis: 13, 23, 35, 66, 67, 157
Killian, James R.: 61, 116
Kingsport Press case: 37

Lambert, Sam: 45; quoted, 43-44
Land Ordinance of 1785: 4
"Leadership and Coordination to Achieve Suitable Scope and Quality in Education": 94
League of Women Voters: 112
Litton Industries: 75-76
"Local control": meaning of, 120
Look-and-say method: 159
Look-and-say readers: 74-75
Los Angeles: 120

McMurrin, Sterling M.: 35
Manpower Development and Training Act of 1962: 5
Massachusetts: 150; school boards in, 125; state-supported public schools, 132-133; Commissioner of Education, 199
Massachusetts, University of: 106
Massachusetts Advisory Council on Education: 116, 166
Massachusetts Education Licensing Board: 175-194
Massachusetts Foreign Languages Association: 190
Massachusetts Institute of Technology: 14; Lincoln Laboratory, 20; Physical Science Study Committee, 13, 60, 61-63, 116, 182
Massachusetts State Advisory Commission: 106-117

Massachusetts State Board of Education: 183
Massachusetts State Department of Education: 91, 107, 184
Mass media: and education, 77-78
Mathematics: and reform groups, 60
Menzies, Ian: 106, 107
"The Mess in Bay State Education": 107-108
Metropolitanism: 132, 133
Meyer, Agnes: 72
Michigan: 33
Michigan, University of: 22
Michigan Association of School Administrators: 41
Mill, John Stuart: 191
Miller, Richard I.: 84
Minnesota: 39, 118-119
Minnesota Mining: 76
Mississippi: 120
Missouri: 33
MITRE: 20
Modern Language Association: 187
Montaigne, Michel: 175
Morrill Land Grant Act of 1862: 4-5

NASA: 20
National Academy of Education: 162
National Academy of Sciences: 162, 186
"National Assessment of Educational Progress": 66-69
National Association of Manufacturers: 78
National Association of Secondary School Principals: 43
National Association of State Boards of Education: 86
National Association of State School Boards: 148
National Center for Citizens in Education: 72-73

National Citizens Commission for the Public Schools: 71
National Citizens Council for Better Schools: 71
National Commission on Accrediting: 53, 56
National Commission on Teacher Education and Professional Standards: 57
National Committee for Support of the Public Schools: 72
National Congress of Parents and Teachers: 70, 101, 148
National Council for Accreditation of Teacher Education: 55, 57-59, 165
National Council of Churches: 76
National Council of Teachers of English: 187
National Defense Education Act of 1958: 5
National Education Association: 26-45, 57, 87, 145, 148, 153; budget of, 28; headquarters of, 29; policies of, 30-45; lobbying of, 32-33; state affiliates of, 33, 96-99; publications of, 33-34; and Office of Education, 34-35; and AFT, 35-36, 38, 41, 43; and "sanctions," 36-37; coercive membership habits of, 38-39; and administrators, 38-41; future of, 43; need to change, 43; and National Assessment of Educational Progress, 69; Educational Policies Commission, 84
National exams: in Europe, 47; and college boards, 49
National Foundation on the Arts and the Humanities: 20
National Governors' Conference: 168
National Merit Scholarship exams: 49

National School Boards Association: 70, 99-100, 148, 172
National Science Foundation: 14, 20, 62
National Teacher Examinations: 128
The NEA Journal: 33
Nebraska: 119, 135
Neighborhood Youth Corps: 20
Newark, N.J.: and AFT, 36
New Hampshire: 116, 135
New Haven, Conn.: 144, 147
"New math": 60
New Trier Township High School District: 151
New York City: AFT in, 36; school board, 120, 123; Catholic institutions in, 121; reorganization in, 131; administration of schools in, 138-139; People's School Board, 154
New York State: control of education in, 87-88; State Education Department, 91; school boards in, 126; tax revenue in, 135; school superintendency in, 143
New York State Board of Regents: 14, 81, 141
New York State Citizens Committee for the Public Schools: 72
New York Times: 7
Nock, Albert Jay: vii
North Central Association of Colleges and Secondary Schools: 53
North Dakota: 91
Northwest Association of Secondary and Higher Schools, 53

Oak Ridge: 20
Office of Economic Opportunity: 19, 20
Office of Emergency Planning: 19
Office of Science and Technology: 19
Ohio: 119

Oklahoma: 37, 99
Oregon Education Association: 97-98
Organization of Educational Research in the U.S.: 17-18
Orwell, George: 198

Parents: and education, 146-154
Passow, A. Harry: 131
Peace Corps: 191
Pennsylvania: 119
"People's School Board": 154
Philadelphia: 121
Philco-Ford: 76
Physical Science Study Committee: 60, 61-63
Politics: of education, viii; and school boards, 123
Poverty: 19, 154
"A Power-Play for Control of Education": 172
Private schools: 121
Professional educators: 156; defined, 14-15; and Office of Education, 16; and government, 22; knowledge of, 158; and laymen, 160-162
President: office of and education, 19-20
President's Science Advisory Committee: 22
Property tax: 134-135
Proposed Standards for State Approval of Teacher Education: 179
PTA: 147, 168, 172; influence in states, 148-149. *See also* National Congress of Parents and Teachers
Public, The: and education, 150
Publishing industry: and education, 74-75; and teaching of reading, 74-75

"Racial Isolation in the Public Schools": 21

Rafferty, Max: 86, 89, 90, 98, 172
Rand Corporation: 20
Raytheon: 76
RCA: 76
Reader's Digest: 76
Reading: teaching of and publishers, 74-75; research in, 159-160; definition of, 198
"Reading Readiness Tests as Predictory of Success in Reading": 16-17
Reading Reform Foundation: 74, 159
Reagan, Ronald: 90
Regional Educational Laboratories: 12-16; and Office of Education, 14-15
Religious groups: and education, 76-77
Research, educational: and Office of Education, 16-19; and schools of education, 18
Rhode Island: 116
Robbins Committee: 8-9
Roman Catholics: 121; in Massachusetts, 106

Sanctions: 36-37
Sanford, Terry: 95
San Francisco Curriculum Survey Committee: 152
San Francisco State College: 152
Scholars: and teacher education, 182; in school affairs, 163
School boards: powers of, 122-130; and politics, 123; and hiring of teachers, 128-129; and finances, 129
School district reorganization: political effects of, 130-137
School finances: 134-135
Schools of education: and research, 18

Science: and curriculum reform groups, 60-63
Science Curriculum Improvement Study: 60
Scotland: power of teachers in, 144
Segregation: and NEA, 41; de facto, 131
Servicemen's Readjustment Act of 1944: 5
Simpson, Roy: 90
Smith-Hughes Act of 1917: 5
Smithsonian Institution: 20
Society of Academic Teachers: 40
South Carolina: 119, 135
South Dakota: 91
Special Advisory Commission on Civil Disorders: 21
Standards and Evaluative Criteria for the Accreditation of Teacher Education: 179
Stanford University, School Mathematics Study Group: 60
State Advisory Commissions: 103-117
State boards of education: 83-91; duties of, 84-85
State departments of education: 91-95
State government: and education, 79-117
State legislatures: 80-83; and research staffs, 82-83
State superintendents of education: 86-87
State taxpayers' associations: 101
State voluntary groups: 95-103
States: teacher influence in, 101-102; influence of PTA, 148-149; and federal money, 168-169
States Rights position: on federal aid, 167
Superintendents, district: 142
Superintendents of schools: power

of, 127, 137-141; education of, 143
Sutton, Willie: 19
Sweden: education ministry in, 8

Taft, Senator Robert: 11
Taxpayers' associations: 150
Taylor, Harold: 72
Teacher education: 179-180
Teacher training: 164
Teachers: in U.S., 25-26; organiza-
tions, 25-45; and educational
policy, 42; of academic subjects
and states, 101; of special sub-
jects and states, 101; hiring of and
school boards, 128-129; power of
local, 137-146; and school policy,
144-146; as experts in education,
163; and teacher education and
certification, 181
Teachers College (Columbia Univer-
sity): 74, 84, 128
Tennessee: 118-119
Testing: changes in, 50-51
Testing Agencies: 47-51
Texas: 119
Time: 75
"A Time to Listen . . . A Time to
Act": 21
Twain, Mark: 122

United Federation of Teachers,
N.Y.: 36, 145
United States: private and church-
related schools in, 120-121
U.S. Census Bureau: "Standard
Metropolitan Statistical Area," 130
U.S. Congress: and education, 4-6;
and general aid, 11-12; and cate-
gorical aid, 11-12
U.S. Court of Appeals, D.C.: 7-8
U.S. Department of Agriculture: 20
U.S. Department of Defense: 22

U.S. Department of Health, Education, and Welfare: 21
U.S. Department of Labor: 20
U.S. Department of State: 20
U.S. Office of Education: 8-24, 171,
179, 191; establishment of, 9;
criticism of, 9-10; statistics of, 9-
10; programs of, 10-11; and educational policy, 11, 19; control by,
12-13; and regional labs, 14-15;
and professional educators, 16; and
research, 16-19; improving of, 23;
and NEA, 34-35; its study of state
departments of education, 94
U.S. Supreme Court: 6-7; reapportionment decision, 81
Urban Service Division: 41
Urban Teachers Corps: 190
Utah: 99; and NEA sanctions, 37

Vermont: 119
Veterans organizations: 78
VISTA: 20, 191
Vocational education: 112
Vocational Education Act of 1963: 5

Wales: 120
Walt Disney Productions: 76
Warren, Earl: 90
Weber, Max: 138
Wesberry v. Sanders: 7
Westinghouse: 75
Wharton, Edith: 18
White House Conference on Educa-
tion: 21, 162; in 1955, 71
Why Johnny Can't Read: 158
Willis, Benjamin C.: 109, 112
Willis-Harrington Act: 184
Willis-Harrington Report: 177
Wisconsin: 39, 120
Wright, J. Skelly: 7-8
Wyoming: 91

Zacharias, Jerrold: 61-62